The World of
Art Nouveau

The World of
Art Nouveau

MARTIN BATTERSBY

Funk & Wagnalls, New York

Contents

Introduction

The 14th of April, 1900, was an anxious day for Alfred Picard. For the last six years since his appointment as Commissioner-General for the greatest Exhibition ever to be held in Paris, he and his assistant Bovard had had an almost daily battle with bureaucracy to achieve his conception of what the most important of the fifteen exhibitions which had taken place in Paris should be — the most important for the reason that it was intended to usher in the new century with a display of French triumphs in every field of science, technology and the arts. Picard had seen an endless procession of ministers appointed, of ministers dismissed, disgraced or forced to resign. Decrees of vital importance to his plans lay for months on official desks, unsigned for reasons of fear of accepting responsibility, or through neglect or indifference, and, if action were taken through his insistence, subject to frustrating alterations and amendments. Some of his plans had met with storms of protest. His project of realising the original idea of Gabriel, the architect of the Place de la Concorde, by opening an avenue stretching from the Invalides on the Left Bank across the Champs de Mars, crossing the Seine by the new Pont Alexandre III — inaugurated by the Czar of Russia in 1896 — and thence into the Champs Elysées would, it was admitted, give Paris a magnificent new vista but it would also necessitate the demolition of the Palais d'Industrie which had housed the 1855 Exhibition. For years this building had been considered an eyesore and a blot on the approach to the Arc de Triomphe, but now that it was threatened with destruction accusations of vandalism were hurled at Picard by the very people who had been loudest in complaining.

In spite of all these delays and upsets, Picard struggled on with quiet persistence, gaining most of his battles and making alternative plans for those he lost — sometimes strategically.

The actual construction of the Exhibition was delayed until 1898 and serious doubts were felt for the opening date of April 15, fixed six years previously — doubts which grew as the winter of 1899–1900 advanced. Picard found he had a new enemy, and one impervious to the methods of guile and persuasion he had developed in his struggles with the ministries. The weather although mild was abnormally wet. For weeks on end most of the enormous site of the Exhibition was waterlogged, delaying the building of the most important pavilions, and work could only be done on those parts of the grounds which sloped down to the Seine and were drained of the rainwater which teemed down for weeks on end. But Picard's unflagging enthusiasm communicated itself to those working under his direction, and despite the delays the vast, elaborate buildings rose at an unprecedented speed. One after another the fantastic structures were completed, looking as solid as though they were to last indefinitely instead of having a life of six months. Huge groups of statuary were hauled into position. Gradually the sea of churned-up mud surrounding them was transformed into lawns and gardens planted with trees and flowers from Japan, Madagascar and every colony of France's possession. Such was the progress made, that the opening date was actually advanced to April 14. The weather had become less inclement — it was too much to hope for that the brilliant sunshine which had lasted throughout the 1889 Exhibition, like a heavenly blessing upon the hundredth anniversary of the French Revolution, would be repeated in 1900. In fact, it was surpassed, and the weather during the duration of the Exhibition was too good. The sun blazed down during the whole summer and the intense heat proved discouraging to a great many visitors. But after the long, wet winter the Inauguration Day dawned without a cloud, and Paris smiled in the clear fresh light of a sunny spring morning.

The opening ceremony was to be performed by the President of the French Republic, M. Emile Loubet, in the Salle des Fêtes which had been created for the occasion inside the Galerie des Machines which, like the Eiffel Tower, had been built for the 1889 Exhibition. While the audience of over twenty thousand people waited in the vast rotunda, they were able to admire the gigantic murals by Cormon, Flameng, Maignan and Rochegrosse representing the industries and products of France. Some of the more nervous recalled that the wings of the building containing the Salle des Fêtes were filled with gaily decorated but highly inflammable booths, and memories were revived of the tragic holocaust three years before at the Charity Bazaar in the Rue Jean-Goujon, when 125 people, mostly women, were burned to death in a few moments. Any such gloomy thoughts were dispelled by the strains of the *Marseillaise* from an orchestra under the direction of M. Taffand, followed by Massanet's *Marche Solonnelle* as the diminutive M. Loubet escorted by his ministers made his way to the platform. The Minister of Commerce and Industry, M. Millerand, stepped forward and launched into a fervent and resounding speech, every word of which was clearly audible throughout the vast auditorium. M. Loubet, so small as to be almost invisible to those in the more distant seats, then made a speech declaring the Exhibition open — a speech which unfortunately was only heard by those in his immediate neighbourhood. This ceremony over, M. Loubet, flanked by M. Millerand and M. Picard, made a short tour on foot and by boat before the President returned to the Elysée Palace. M. Picard was no doubt fully occupied for the rest of this momentous day with officials, but he must have paused to look round at the culmination of six years' work with pride. Later he would hear criticisms that the buildings themselves were reactionary in design and that the advances in technique, which had been a characteristic of the 1889 Exhibition, had not been taken advantage of or used as might have been expected. Antonin Proust considered that the buildings were old-fashioned in comparison with those in the previous exhibition and regretted that iron, which he considered destined to transform the architecture of the future, was not used to a greater extent — that the lesson of the Eiffel Tower and the Palais du Trocadéro had not been assimilated. The Exhibition was intended, the critics pointed out, to herald the twentieth century, although there had been heated arguments as to whether the year 1900 belonged properly to the nineteenth or to the twentieth century, but the prevailing influence in the designs of the major buildings such as the Palais de l'Electricité, the Chateau d'Eau and the Industrial Pavilions along the Esplanade des Invalides was mainly baroque and in fact a great many of the architects would have appeared to have drawn their inspiration from the more elaborate designs for stage settings by the Bibbiena family — this excludes the pavilions built in the national style of the countries they represented. Underneath the fantastic proliferation of ornament there were frameworks of iron girders as photographs taken while the work was in progress indicate, but this was used simply for speed, convenience and economy.

But this lack of vision, this failure to grasp the opportunities offered by new mediums, does not seem to have disturbed any but a few critics, and for the greater part it was agreed that an effect of great beauty had been achieved both in the design and layout of the buildings and in the decorative use of trees and flowers. Unfortunately, little imagination was used in the illumination of the buildings after dark. Ordinary street lights were placed at intervals in the avenues and esplanades; one or two buildings, the entrance in the Place de la Concorde, the Palais de l'Electricité, had electric light bulbs incorporated into the design, and of course the Eiffel Tower was outlined in electricity, the use of which was still, however, undeveloped and it is interesting to speculate what magnificent effects could have been obtained had more modern techniques of flood-lighting been available in 1900. The poor general lighting of the Exhibition was a contributory factor to the low attendance figures during the evenings, but even during the daytime the Exhibition was rarely crowded as the area covered by the Exhibition was so great that even the greatest

crowds could move about in comfort. According to one estimate, the average attendance figure was two thousand per day,
but this figure seems improbably low. Even so, it began to be
realised that the Exhibition would result in a considerable
financial loss. That of 1867 had made nearly a million francs
profit, a sum exceeded by the 1889 exhibition; no figures were
published for the one held in 1878 and the balance-sheets
were described enigmatically as 'curious and instructive'. The
fears about the weather had, as has been described, been
groundless. In fact, the weather was so fine as to be a disad-
vantage. To cross on foot the Pont Alexandre III to get from
one section to the other on the opposite side of the Seine was a
daunting experience for the bridge offered no shelter from the
blazing sunshine. One unfortunate result of the excessively
warm weather was that the entertainments which formed part
of the Exhibition were almost deserted for the evening performances, spelling near ruin for the impresarios who had taken
concessions. Both Parisians and tourists found it more comfortable to spend their evening out of doors, patronising the
cafés along the Grand Boulevards rather than covering the
enormous vistas of the Exhibition and sitting in small and
often ill-ventilated theatres watching feverish displays of
native dancing. Loïe Fuller, for instance, having undertaken
the responsibility for presenting the celebrated Japanese
actress Sada Yacco, found that in spite of the ecstatic notices
which her protégée had received from the critics, the
audiences were too sparse to begin to meet the cost of production, with the result that she had to undergo a long and
exhausting tour of Germany after the close of the Exhibition
in order to recoup her losses. Nightly the belly-dancers, the
painted adolescents and the Negroes at the Egyptian Theatre
drove themselves into frenzies performing strange, exotic
dances — never before seen in Europe — to a handful of spec-
tators. Visitors preferred to linger in the cool shades of the
nearby Japanese gardens with their beds of peonies, iris and
hortensia set among dwarfed pine trees, or to sip tea in the
Ceylon Pavilion — which had somehow acquired a reputation as
a favourite haunt of those in search of adventure in the traditional hours of five and seven. English visitors in need of

nothing more than a good cup of tea were catered for at the English Restaurant, which bore a close resemblance to a sports pavilion and was liberally plastered with signs announcing 'Teas' and 'Cold Luncheons'.

Fortunately, walking was not the only means of transport from one part of the Exhibition grounds to another. Less energetic visitors could use the 'Trottoir Roulant'—confidently described as the pavement of the future. This covered a considerable area and provided easy access to the main attractions. Suspended some twenty feet in the air, it consisted of three parallel sections, one stationary, one moving very slowly, and a third which was much wider and rattled along at eight kilometres an hour. Each section was raised about six inches higher than its neighbour to obviate the danger of the trailing dresses of the women becoming tangled. It soon became a favourite pastime to stand on the fixed platform and watch the trepidation of the more unsophisticated visitors, especially those from the provinces to whom anything in Paris was a novelty, as they timidly stepped on the slow section and then, gaining confidence, moved on to the faster one. Many complaints were made that no seating accommodation had been provided for the elderly or the

infirm, and that no protection had been given against rain or shade from the ever-blazing sun.

The main entrance to the Exhibition was in the Place de la Concorde. However, this was not used on the Opening Day by M. Loubet and the official party—a smaller entrance more conveniently within reach of the Elysée Palace was preferred, much to the chagrin of the architect, M. Binet, who considered that he and his monumental gateway had been slighted. Rene Binet had designed a fantastically ornamental archway flanked by two decorative pylons, and supporting 'La Parisienne,' a colossal statue by

Moreau-Gauthier who, instead of depicting a conventional goddess, muse or a figure in classical costume representing the City of Paris, had elected to personify the spirit of the Exhibition as a contemporary women in modern dress — an idea which caused a great amount of controversy and even derision. The base of this monumental entrance was ornamented with two bands of sculpture both executed ih enamelled faince by the firm of Muller, the lower band of animals modelled in relief by a sixteen-year-old sculptor, Paul Jouve, the upper and more important section having as its subject 'Le Travail' after originals by Guillot. Above this base rose the arches of the entrance, also faced in coloured faience on a metal foundation with electric light bulbs incorporated into the design. The siting of this entrance was a boon for Maxime Gaillard, who had opened a small bistro for coachmen in the Rue Royale in 1892. Realising that the close proximity of the new entrance would benefit him, he hastily redecorated his premises in the latest style, discouraged his former clients, and before long the premises acquired a rather raffish reputation under the name of 'Maxim's'.

Once through Binet's entrance the visitor might well have been bewildered by the number of pavilions on both sides of the river. Significantly, the place of honour had been given to the Russian Pavilion for political reasons. Both France and Russia distrusted Germany and the alliance between the two countries, it was confidently anticipated, would curb the ambitions of the German Emperor who was not only detested as representing the country which had humiliated France in the war of 1870 — the annexation of Alsace and parts of Lorraine was never to be forgotten by any patriotic Frenchman — but was also disliked personally. There had been no lack of enthusiasm in the circulation of stories of his sadistic performances in the brothels of Paris. The Czar, accompanied by the Czarina — herself of German origin although that fact was never mentioned — had paid a State visit to Paris in 1896 to open the Pont Alexandre III, named in honour of the Royal visitor's grandfather, and the Royal couple had made an impression on the Parisians in spite of the fact that neither the Czar nor the Czarina were ever seen to smile and the Czarina had a reputation of being extremely prudish. However, she was well dressed, which is more than could be said for the German Empress, whose clothes were only remarkable for their inexpensiveness. Once again the Russian rulers made the trip to Paris for the opening of the Russian pavilion, and during the ceremony M. Loubet was presented with a large map of France made from rare marbles, and the principal cities and towns indicated by precious stones. This was reputed to have taken four years to make. Unfortunately, the Russian Pavilion was not completed and the Panorama representing a trip on the Trans-Siberian railway, which was intended to be one of the main attractions of the exhibit, was not installed. There was some consolation in the fact that the German Pavilion was in an even more unfinished condition, for the organisers had expressed dissatisfaction at the area allotted to them and had demanded and received an extension. There is no record of their pavilion being opened by the French President.

The English artist and connoisseur, Charles Ricketts, recording his visit on May 23 describes 'a wild scamper through the Universal Exhibition. We missed our entrance and wandered through miles of glaring modern rubbish. The sculpture had sunk to an even lower level than the painting. The English section is singularly lifeless.' The whole question of the English section had proved a problem necessitating the use of the greatest diplomacy and tact. Relations between France and England had been extremely strained for some years, especially during the six years of preparation for the Exhibition, and on at least two occasions diplomatic relations were on the verge of being broken off completely. The culmination had come in 1898 when in spite of warnings from Whitehall that any penetration of the Nile Valley would be regarded as a hostile act, the French had sent an expeditionary force led by Colonel Marchand as far as Fashoda, a small town of great strategic importance. Kitchener set out with a superior force and no definite instructions from Whitehall, but knowing full well that any false move would precipitate a conflict between the two countries. The situation was finally settled by the withdrawal of Marchand's entirely inadequate force, but it was regarded as a humiliation for France—a feeling fostered by the press of both countries who had whipped up patriotic fervour on both sides and had almost frustrated the efforts of those who realised the dangers of anything less than a peaceful settlement. The name 'Fashoda' was removed from all French atlases and school text books, and was replaced by that of Kodok. Possibly in retaliation, the French more or less openly sided with the Boers in the South African conflict, and it was no secret that Paris was a rallying point for Irish volunteers for the Boer forces. Much space was given in the French newspapers to the marriage of the Irish writer, beauty and patriot Maud Gonne to Major MacBride, who was described as a 'hero of the siege of Ladysmith.' The alliance between France and Russia for the purpose of enclosing their common enemy Germany was regarded with suspicion in England, although Germany was not noted for any friendly feelings for England. Altogether, it would have been preferable if some excuse could have been found for not participating in the Exhibition, as had been done in the case of the Exhibition of 1889 when the official reason for abstaining was that as the Exhibition was to commemorate the hundredth anniversary of the French Revolution, the occasion was purely French. But this time no such argument could be put forward, and although many people in England would have preferred to do so, it was not considered advisable entirely to boycott the exhibition when practically every other country in the world was participating. Such a step would only have served to deepen the breach between the two countries. Finally, a face-saving compromise was found, and probably the credit for this was due to the influence of the Prince of Wales who was a constant visitor to Paris, and was personally popular with the Parisians. There would be no official pavilion with displays of British products or of, to use a later phrase, the British way of life. Instead, there would be a version by Lutyens, rather oddly constructed of steel and concrete, of a seventeenth-century building, Kingston House, which was furnished with antique furniture, tapestries and paintings. Situated in the Rue des Nations it was, officially at least, intended as a residence for the Prince of Wales on his visits to the Exhibition.

Whether in fact he ever used it is not recorded, but it was highly improbable as the Rue des Nations was criticised as being cramped and noisy and would hardly have afforded the Prince the privacy which was most necessary on his expeditions to Paris. Kingston House was open to the public for inspection but its contents, chosen as being among the finest examples of English art of the seventeenth and eighteenth centuries, had little interest for the French who had no admiration for English art of any period. Various London firms of decorators and furnishers had exhibits in the commercial sections of the Exhibition, but these were private efforts and were not under official sponsorship. There were adverse criticisms of the official policy in the English press, as it was felt that an opportunity had been lost for England to show the work of her designers and craftsmen, and the work of the Arts and Crafts Society, for instance, was not represented.

Charles Ricketts' comments on the sculpture were not entirely unjustified, for all the buildings were decorated with sculptured groups and reliefs wherever space could be found to accommodate them, and the interior of the Grand Palais, which was entirely devoted to French art of the nineteenth century, closely resembled a cemetery. The Grand Palais itself seems to have been unfortunate from its conception, being considered to have been badly designed, and its inauguration by the indefatigable M. Loubet was disastrous. The arrangements for the reception of the three thousand guests broke down as it was not announced that only those with invitations would be admitted, and the number of guests was more than doubled by members of the public who saw no reason why they should be refused admission; in the resulting chaos, the Presidential party were locked out as well as the gate-crashers.

Its neighbour, the Petit Palais, was on the contrary the greatest possible success. The building received unreserved praise and was considered worthy of Gabriel, the great architect of the eighteenth century. The exhibition it housed, that of French art from the earliest times to 1800, was admired not only for the high quality of the exhibits but also for the elegant manner in which they were displayed. Regrets were

expressed that the exhibits could not have been permanently
on display, and that after six months they would be dispersed
and the building handed over to the Beaux Arts. M. Molinier,
the director of the Louvre, had wisely decided not to borrow
from the museums and galleries of Paris, thus depleting the
collections which would be visited by the tourists flocking to
Paris that summer. Instead, he had persuaded private collectors and the museums and galleries of not only provincial
France, but also of Belgium, Italy and Germany, to lend their
finest pieces, thus giving foreign visitors as well as the French
themselves the opportunity of seeing collected together some
of the glories of French creative inspiration of all periods.
Nothing, incidentally, was borrowed from England where
some of the finest pieces of French eighteenth-century furniture and painting had found their way in the years following
the French Revolution.

For those less interested in the Fine Arts, the Colonial
Section gave the most cause for national pride and satisfaction.
This was grouped around the Palais du Trocadéro, a relic of
the previous exhibition of 1889, and since that date the number of French colonies had considerably increased, notably by
the addition of Madagascar — again an acquisition not welcome to England as that strange, mysterious island was so
strategically placed that it could menace the route to India. In
1885 the French had negotiated the Treaty of Tamatave,
which gave them rights to the port of Diego Suarez as well as
diplomatic rights. Two years previously, Queen Ranavalona
III had in a double ceremony been crowned and married to
the Prime Minister Rain Ilaiarivony, the former husband of
the two preceding queens, one of whom was a cousin of
Ranavalona. The groom, who must be unique in having no
less than three royal spouses, proved less successful in dealing
with the French who in 1895 under the pretext of bad will on
the part of the Malagays, sent a punitive expedition. The
island was declared a protectorate, and in the following year a
colony. Ranavalona was deposed, exiled first to Réunion and
then to Algiers where she died in 1917. She had always been
dressed by Worth and her allowance was sufficient for her to
continue to do so, and she could often be seen in Paris when

she came to order clothes, an aristocratic but melancholy figure dressed in the height of fashion and accompanied by the one lady-in-waiting allowed her as a token of her vanished rank. The great silver vases from the Silver Palace at Tananarive, the state robes of the deposed monarch, and the regalia were removed to Paris 'for safety', and were to be seen in the Madagascan Pavilion where specimens of gold, lead, rare woods, rubber, coffee, tobacco, vanilla and rice demonstrated the richness of the natural products of the new colony, and explained the desirability of its coming under the protection of France. Queen Ranavalona's Royal Orchestra, some twenty musicians, including a saxophone player, all dressed in white robes with striped scarves and straw hats and clearly showing in their features the mixture of Negro, Arab, Malay and Polynesian strains characteristic of the natives of Madagascar, became great favourites and a number from their repertoire, '*Ah! Zut alors! Si ta sœur est malade . . .*' — a title reminiscent of Ronald Firbank — became very popular with Parisians. An attempt was made to create the atmosphere of a Madagascan forest on an island in the ornamental lake of the Trocadero but the project was not a success as the snakes and crocodiles which were an essential part of the effect took badly to their exile and died.

Picard had had even greater frustrations with the Colonial Section than with any other part of the Exhibition, and the authorisation to start work there was only signed after the Budget in June 1899. Despite this delay, the Colonial exhibits were ready ahead of time as much of the building had already been prefabricated in their countries of origin and it was only necessary to erect them *in situ*, where they were inhabited by the native craftsmen and dancers and their families. Visitors could marvel at the copy of a Tonkinese palace, a complete Annamite village, a Cambodian white elephant named Chérie, pagodas from Cochin-China and Indo-China, replicas complete with tropical plants of Khmer ruins, jewellers and weavers from Senegal, ivory from the Congo, the thrones of the Kings of Dahomey and gold from Guinea and the Ivory Coast. The older colonies of the West Indies were not such a novelty to Parisians but the exhibits from Tahiti among the colonies in the Pacific attracted a great many visitors who had admired Pierre Loti's successful novels set in that island.

Equally exotic were the exhibits in the Rue des Nations where a number of countries had pavilions depicting with varying degrees of success the characteristic national architecture and housing works of art and products of the country. It was a strange medley of buildings with frontages on the Rue des Nations and on the Seine whose banks had been built out to provide landing stages for the boats which provided a means of getting from one end of the vast exhibition grounds to the other. A portion of Old Nuremburg was placed next to a Javanese Palace, a Turkish kiosk had as neighbours reproductions of famous but vanished buildings of mediaeval Paris, which served as shops where the souvenirs and guides to the Exhibition were on sale.

Of all the buildings there were three in particular with which we shall be concerned. One, approximately on the site of the present Air Terminal on the Esplanade des Invalides, was devoted to Art Nouveau, and while not attempting to trace the history of that fascinating style, an attempt will be made to throw some light on the creator of that building, S. Bing, and on the circle of people he knew who influenced him and whom in turn he influenced. Secondly, an enchanting tiny theatre close to the Rodin exhibit on the opposite bank of the Seine, which was created as a setting for Loïe Fuller whose adventurous life will be described; and lastly, another theatre in the Colonial section where the greatest beauty of the day performed her dances. Bing was the major impresario of Art Nouveau, Loïe Fuller its living embodiment and together with Cléo de Mérode the source of inspiration for artists and designers.

Peonies and Fleur-de-lis

Art Nouveau could not have come into being as a decorative style without the inspiration of Japanese art. Constantly in contemporary sources there are references to the influence of Japan and to the debt owed to that country's craftsmen by French designers. Chinese art had long been familiar to the West since Roman times but it was not until the middle of the sixteenth century that a band of Portuguese under the leadership of Francis Xavier arrived in Japan, were made a grant of land and succeeded in converting a number of Japanese to Christianity. The Japanese who at that time were under the leadership of a feudal warlord with no religious beliefs and a deep hatred of Buddhism, were tolerant of the attempts to convert them to Christianity and for some fifty years the Portuguese were the only Europeans to reside in Japan, living in an atmosphere of mutual trust and respect. The arrival of the Spanish in 1600 sparked off a considerable amount of resentment among the Portuguese who were not only antagonistic to their European neighbours but were in addition suspicious of the large number of Spanish friars among the new arrivals. In the same year the Englishmen Will Adams landed in Japan and made such a favourable impression on the overlord Ieyasu by his advice on maritime matters that he was not allowed to leave Japan, married a Japanese and died without ever seeing his native country again. Through Adams' influence, permission was granted for both the

English and the Dutch to establish trading posts — the
English abandoned theirs after ten years of unprofitable trading — and both countries acquired reputations for honesty and
fair dealing which were not shared by the Spanish and
Portuguese, who not only indulged in bitter feuds among
themselves but made as much trouble as possible for their
Protestant rivals. The strife and mischief-making became so
intense that Ieyasu no doubt on the advice of Adams passed a
decree in 1614 banishing all priests from Japan. This decree
was enforced with the utmost severity. Ieyasu was succeeded
in 1616 by his son Hidetada, and the Christian missionaries
found themselves hounded with even greater ferocity — a
necessary step as considerable numbers of Spanish priests
were smuggling themselves into the country in disguise and
fomenting trouble, and it was discovered that they were taking
the sinister step of making maps. Matters came to a head in
1637 when all foreigners were banished from Japan with the
exception of the Dutch, who were allowed to establish a trading post on the small island of Deshima in the harbour of
Nagasaki. In addition, no Japanese were allowed to leave the
country, which was then virtually cut off from the rest of the
world except for the strictly controlled outlet offered by the
Dutch at Deshima, through which came a certain amount of
Japanese artifacts, mostly lacquer and porcelain. Madame de
Pompadour had a number of pieces of Japanese lacquer
mounted in ormolu in her apartments at Versailles and small
panels of lacquer were incorporated into Dutch furniture at
the end of the eighteenth century. Japanese porcelain was
brought to Europe in considerable quantities, particularly
during the early 1700s and the decorative motifs on them,
notably those on the porcelain from the Arita factory, were
widely imitated in Europe.

This state of mediaeval seclusion was to last for over two
hundred years until it crumbled before the expansion and
colonial ambitions of the European countries and Japan was
forced at the point of the gun to enter the nineteenth century.
Her geographical position was mainly responsible for this.
Russia was in the process of colonising Eastern Siberia and
Alaska, and Japan, situated between the two territories, could

be a source of danger to both. Britain having defeated China in the Opium Wars was looking for more markets to absorb her increasing output of consumer goods. America was interested in the possibilities of trade with Japan and needed bases where her ships of the Pacific whaling fleets could be refuelled. Each country, desirous of being the first on the field, put increasing pressure on Japan in the form of gunboats, but it was the American Commander Perry who forced the Japanese to sign a treaty with America, in March 1854. A few months later the Japanese signed a similar treaty with the British who were in the throes of the Crimean War and thus gained an advantage over the Russians. By 1858 Japan had signed treaties with all the major powers in Europe including France. England was too occupied in India to pay much attention to Japan, America was engaged in the Civil War, but France took the opportunity offered of extending her sphere of influence in the Far East and assisted Japan's entry into the modern world by sending French technicians and advisers. Considerable financial aid was granted to the Japanese by the French Government for the establishment of heavy industries, while Japanese students, permitted to leave the country for the first time in two hundred years, flocked to Paris to learn French, and to acquire the knowledge and skills of the West. In 1867 the Japanese contributed to the Paris Exhibition, sending a number of works of art in addition to commercial products.

There were already shops in Paris selling Chinese works of art and a trickle of Japanese objects gradually began to appear — goods obtained from Japan by Chinese traders. Before a thorough knowledge of Japanese art was common it is probable that there was no difference to Western eyes between the artifacts of both countries, but a greater familiarity with Japanese idioms of ornament and with the Japanese language made connoisseurs aware of the individuality of the products of the newly opened country.

The objects which were mostly stocked in the late 'sixties and the 'seventies in the various Japanese shops seem to have been those which could be brought on the lengthy voyage from the Far East without too much risk of damage and were mostly small in dimension, Ivory and wood 'netsuké, the

elaborately carved toggles used to fasten a tobacco pouch or
the medicine boxes called 'inro' to the belt, were usually no
more than an inch or an inch and a half in diameter, and a
large number of these could be packed into a fairly small
space. Small lacquer boxes could be easily transported, as
could books of drawings. Sword guards or tsuba occupied
little space, and vast numbers of these were imported into
France — usually the later and more elaborate specimens in
bronze decorated with gold or silver. The earlier examples in
iron were not at first appreciated, but as connoisseurs became
more used to the strange decorative ideals of Japanese art, the
simplicity and strength of the earlier designs found admirers.
But most eagerly sought after were the 'fousakas', squares of
material used in Japan to cover a gift no matter how trivial.
The most prized specimens had been made at Kyoto, the
ancient capital of Japan, but later examples were made at
Togane. They were of various materials; silk, velvet or cotton
with embroidered, woven or painted decorations. The finest
collection in Paris was reported to belong to a M. Lansyer.
Usually they were framed and hung on the walls as pictures or
incorporated in firescreens, but more often than not they were
used as cushion covers.

'A La Porte Chinoise' in the Rue Vivienne was opened in
1855, and in addition to being a teashop sold Oriental objects,
at first Chinese, but later, as the trade treaty with Japan
became effective, Japanese works of art were available to the
public. It was then that in June 1861, Edmond de Goncourt
(or it may have been his brother Jules — at that time they were
both compiling their journal but writing as one person)
bought a number of Japanese drawings which aroused great
enthusiasm when shown to his circle of friends. Like
'L'Empire du Mikado', which specialised in cheap Japanese
toys and novelties, 'A La Porte Chinoise' lacked the
attraction of the shop in the Rue de Rivoli owned by
Madame de Soye, an enormously fat woman with an unusually white skin, who presided over her exotic kingdom like
a barbaric idol, covered in a mass of jewellery which
glittered and tinkled with the coquettish gestures which
beguiled the writers, painters and poets who were her clients.

She had lived for some years in Japan and it was said that her extraordinary appearance, combined with her administration of quinine during an epidemic, earned her from her grateful patients the reputation of being the Virgin Mary. But Madame de Soye's amiability had its limits, however, and was never allowed to interfere with her business acumen. The sculptor Zachari Astruc asked her to reserve a splendid Japanese fan for him, promising to return to pay for it. After a time, Madame de Soye decided she had waited long enough

and sold it to Whistler. Unfortunately, the two men met at a dinner party the same evening. Astruc became so enraged when Whistler innocently described his new purchase, and he realised that it was the identical fan that had been reserved for him, that he threatened to black Whistler's eye and the other guests had to intervene to stop a fight.

It was at Madame de Soye's shop that admirers of Japanese art found they could discover more than a new work of art and that a mutual admiration for a fine bronze or piece of lacquer was as good as an introduction to a charming stranger — a trend which spread to other establishments of the same nature, and must have been a source of irritation to the proprietors when they found themselves with a shop full of customers more interested in each other than in the objects on display — customers who came singly and left in pairs.

La Maison Sichel, run by two brothers Philippe and Auguste Sichel, was already enjoying a reputation for selling eighteenth-century French furniture of very fine quality when the Sichels decided in the early 'seventies to include Japanese objects of equally high standard, and in a short time La Maison Sichel took its place among the foremost dealers in this genre — also acquiring the reputation of being a convenient meeting place for those in search of adventure.

Philippe Sichel, like many of the other dealers, spent a considerable time in Japan and visited that country before Bing. He shrewdly kept back for his own enjoyment the first pieces that came into his possession and his collection was valued at 300,000 francs.

The most notable Parisian dealer in Japanese works of art was undoubtedly Bing, about whom personally little is known except that he was Jewish and of German origin. Even his first name is conjectural, as he was usually referred to as 'S. Bing'. The alternatives of Siegfried and Samuel have been given, and possibly he was known first as Siegfried, but finding that such a noticeably German name was not popular in Paris so soon after the French defeat in the Franco-Prussian War, he may have changed it to Samuel, only to find that the anti-semitism which could have driven him from Germany was as rampant in France, and he compromised by using the initial. The books and articles which he wrote are always signed 'S. Bing' and he is invariably referred to in that way. The date of his arrival in Paris from Hamburg is again uncertain, but was certainly before July 1, 1875, when Edmond de Goncourt, in company with his friend Philippe Sichel, visited Bing's shop in the Rue Chauchat to see his new shipment from the Orient being unpacked. The fact that it was a new shipment, and that the place was crowded with people, suggests that Bing was already well established and that dealers and collectors were eagerly awaiting the arrival of new merchandise.

In addition to the volume of drawings he had bought at 'A La Porte Chinoise' in 1861, an exhibition of Japanese art in 1867 had aroused de Goncourt's interest and curiosity, but he and his brother Jules were so absorbed in the eighteenth century that the idea of collecting did not occur to him. But the death of his brother Jules, from whom he had never been separated, left a gap in his life which could not be filled in the first torments of grief. He began to find consolation in the study of this strange, exotic civilisation which offered such possibilities of discovery, a civilisation which he perceived with growing fascination was, at times, infinitely more sophisticated and refined than any in the West, even France in the eighteenth century which hitherto he and his brother had regarded as the most elegant.

Sichel and de Goncourt had already had their appetites for Japanese curiosities whetted by having luncheon with Henri Cernuschi and viewing his collection, some fifteen hundred objects of which had been exhibited in the Palais de l'Industrie the previous September (1874) and although they found much to admire among the bronzes, the porcelains, ivories and smaller objects they found less interesting. On leaving Cernuschi they visited the customs stores where a quantity of antiquities, mostly Chinese, were awaiting collection by their owners among whom was Isaac de Camondo and various members of the Rothschild family. By the time they arrived at Bing's shop in the late afternoon, de Goncourt was tired and hungry, but not too much so to lose his head completely over the beautiful objects he saw and he bought a number of pieces, spending a sleepless night wondering how he was going to find the thousand francs to pay for them.

This visit was the first of many, and for the next twenty years de Goncourt made a habit of spending an hour or two in Bing's shop whenever he had time to spare, and after a tiring day doing research for his books on the eighteenth-century French art he would find it a refreshing distraction to browse around Bing's stock and perhaps find some small precious object which he would take from his pocket during his solitary dinners, looking at it in the hollow of his hand. His only regret at having given up smoking was that the pleasure of examining some new Japanese acquisitions was made more exquisite by lighting a cigar or a cigarette at the same time.

He did not, of course, always purchase anything during those visits, but often mentioned something he had noticed as being of particular interest to a friend. Philippe Burty, a critic and an ardent champion of Japanese art, was not, de Goncourt considered, aware of the beauties of Satsuma porcelain and he urged him to look at three particularly fine specimens at Bing's. Burty was equally enthusiastic about the vases and bought them, rather to de Goncourt's annoyance, for he had almost decided to add them to his collection. Bing would often send a message to de Goncourt when he had something particularly fine in the shop, and the latter was one of the first to see a collection of thirty swordguards which had just arrived from Japan, and which de Goncourt declared to be the finest collection of ironwork the world had ever seen. On another occasion he was tempted by two magnificent lacquer boxes, one of gold lacquer signed by Korin and decorated with sprays of chrysanthemum with centres of mother-of-pearl, both of which he purchased for the considerable sum of 2,500 francs.

Previously, Edmond de Goncourt had put one of his purchases to a practical but melancholy use. He had a pet hen, snowy white, thoroughly spoiled and not unintelligent, which was called Blanche and had the liberty of the house. During the Siege of Paris the food situation became extremely acute as the Prussians surrounded and shelled the city. All the edible animals, including an elephant, in the Jardin des Plantes were slaughtered to be eaten, and the chefs of the restaurants exercised their skill in making rats, cats and dogs palatable. Finally the day came in the de Goncourt household when Blanche had to be sacrificed. The servants refused to be involved in the death of the household pet and the master faced the fact that he alone had to perform the deed or there would be no dinner that night. Knowing the importance that the Japanese attributed to their swords which were regarded almost as sacred objects, he decided that as Blanche could not perform an honourable hari-kiri herself, he would use the finest sword in his collection to despatch the innocent bird. After a scene too harrowing to describe, poor Blanche was ready for plucking and cooking by the weeping cook, but she had a subtle revenge — she was so tough as to be completely uneatable.

Edmond de Goncourt, as he describes in *La Maison d'un Artiste*, devoted several rooms to his Japanese collection, but made no attempt to reproduce a Japanese interior. He would probably have regarded as excessive the decoration in the Japanese manner created in 1898 by Mortimer Mempes, an Australian artist of unnoticeable talent, who installed himself in number 25 Cadogan Gardens, a corner house designed by Arthur Haygate Macmurdo in a manner reminiscent of the houses bordering the canals of Amsterdam. All the woodwork of the interior and practically all the furniture was imported from Japan, having been specially made by craftsmen working from traditional designs under Mempes' supervision. The ceilings were elaborately carved, painted and gilded on the lines of those found in Japanese temples; the walls as a contrast were of plain panels of silk or paper; a plain thick carpet was substituted for the Japanese straw matting, which was soon found to be impractical, and Macmurdo's windows were concealed behind lattice work and paper sliding panels. Concessions had to be made with regard to the furniture, no Japanese equivalent of pieces necessary to Western ideas of comfort being in existence, so Chinese hardwood tables and lacquered chairs were used — the latter afterwards proved to be too uncomfortable and occidental upholstered dining chairs and settees were substituted. The lighting was concealed in Japanese lanterns, to harmonise with the decorations, and in addition to a collection of bronzes and lacquer-work, Mempes decorated the dining room with a number of pieces of porcelain he had himself painted in a Japanese factory — bowls and vases of gourd shapes decorated with panels of Japanese subjects in the European manner. If they have survived, these ceramics will pose many a problem to art historians of the future.

Bing's customers included most of the celebrities of the day, including Sarah Bernhardt, who was noticed by de

Goncourt in 1877 wandering round the shop, a long, very pale figure, wrapped in a shapeless and 'interminable' waterproof, picking up, examining and putting down various objects, murmuring to herself, 'That will do for my sister.' On occasion, owing to the precarious financial situation in which she passed most of her life, she was obliged to part with her treasures to meet the demands of her creditors, and in 1884, on the day of the first performance of *Theodora*, she wrote to Cernuschi, whose collection became the Musée Cernuschi on his death, to ask him if he would buy from her a bronze tiger which she had purchased from Bing for 6,000 francs, but which she would sacrifice for half the sum.

In spite of the frequent contacts between Bing and de Goncourt, the dealer-customer relationship never blossomed into a friendship, although they met at the dinners given by 'Les Japonisants' which were meetings of collectors, critics, artists and dealers.

Lévy, one of Bing's assistants who was a specialist in Japanese prints, would give de Goncourt valuable information about Hokusai or Utamaro for an article, but neither he nor his employer seem to have set foot in de Goncourt's home. The reason for this does little credit to de Goncourt. The journals kept by him and his brother Jules, fascinating as they are as records of the social, literary and artistic life of Paris over a period of forty-five years, are flawed by the anti-semitism which particularly after Jules's death in 1870 became an obsession with the surviving brother — lonely in spite of his wide circle of friends and acquaintances. Increasingly he indulges in diatribes, couched in insulting terms, against any Jewish acquaintances who might quite unwittingly have offended him. Distasteful as they may seem in the present day, it would not have been considered so nearly a hundred years ago, and accounts of the Dreyfus case give a revealing picture of the extent of anti-semitism in France during the 'nineties. Sarah Bernhardt, the victim of a vicious caricature by Puck entitled *La Danäe Juive*, wrote a letter of sympathy to Madame Dreyfus and this gesture was generally held to be responsible, according to a writer in *The Illustrated London News*, for the inordinate delays in the grant-

ing of the official honours which she, as the leading actress of France and the possessor of international fame, had every right to expect. It is disconcerting to find reproduced in a newly founded English art magazine a poster designed by Adolph Willette, 'the poetical delineator of Montmartre' for his own electoral campaign when he offered himself in 1889 as the anti-semite candidate for the ninth arrondissement of Paris — a district which included the Rue de Provence where Bing's shop was situated. He drew the Spirit of France as a buxom lady in Gaullish dress, nude to the waist and with a cock's tail attached to her cross-gartered leggings, surmounting a barricade and blowing a trumpet to exhort a number of followers, a workman with a hammer, a Pierrot artist armed with a rifle, a veteran of the Franco-Prussian War and a bearded Gaul who holds on a spear the heads of a pig and a top-hatted financier, while spurning underfoot a broken stone slab entitled 'The Talmud'. The text exhorts Frenchmen to arise and fight the tyranny of the Jewish enemy, fifty thousand of whom have made thirty million Frenchmen their trembling slaves. There is no record that Willette was successful in his political ambitions, but it is nevertheless surprising to find his poster reproduced in *The Studio* for 1893 as an illustration for an article by Charles Hyatt on the collecting of posters and the information that a collector could obtain a copy for three and a half francs.

By 1889 the shadow of the coming storm can be seen in de Goncourt's tart comments that Bing had only modern stuff in his shop and that if he should have anything good or old it was priced too highly — comments which developed into accusations of actual sharp practice on the part of Bing. In 1890 Bing was awarded an official decoration by the Japanese Government for his services in propagating knowledge of Japanese art in the West, another cause for acid remarks from de Goncourt.

At this point in the story another figure emerges to play his part in the tragi-comedy of the relations between the two men.

Tadamara Hayashi's father was a servant employed in Japan by a Dutch doctor who had taught the boy enough Dutch to read a book about Napoleon, who had inspired such an admiration in the young Japanese that his one ambition was to visit the country where his hero had lived. One step towards achieving this ambition was obviously to learn French, which he managed to do, and his chance came when he was offered the post of assistant on the strength of his command of the French language, when the Japanese had an exhibit of works of art in the 1878 Exhibition. At the close of the Exhibition, he stayed on to arrange for the sale of the Japanese exhibit and made his home in France, where he stayed until his death in 1906, apart from lengthy trips to purchase antiquities in Japan. He very soon became known as an authority on Japanese art, and was often commissioned by Bing to purchase on his behalf. In 1887 he went to Japan via America in search of the lacquer and embroideries which were so much in demand in Paris, and from Japan he sent a number of peony plants of types never before seen in Europe to de

Binet: the main entrance to the 1900 Exhibition in the Place de la Concorde.

Fernand Khnopff: mask in tinted ivory, bronze and enamel. Exhibited at the Brussels Exhibition 1897. This mask formed part of the decorations of the studio Khnopff built for his own use in Brussels.

Mastroianni: 'Triomphe de la Jeunesse'. The popularity of postcards taken from tableaux modelled by Mastroianni continued for a number of years after the Art Nouveau style had fallen out of favour. The example reproduced was sent in 1916 to a French soldier in a German prisoner of war camp.

Frank Brangwyn: study for the frescoes on the exterior of
'L'Art Nouveau' 22 Rue de Provence, Paris.

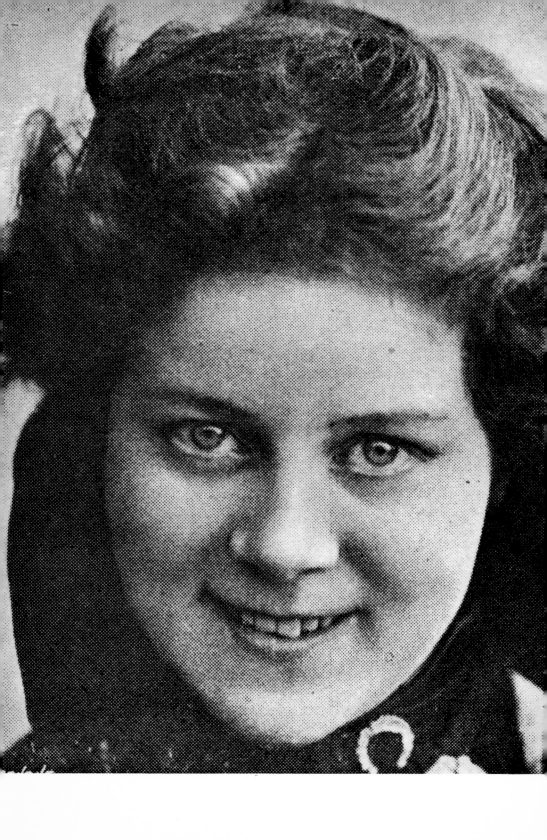

Loïe Fuller: photograph by Bourne.

Eugène Colonna: chair designed for the salon at
'L'Art Nouveau'. Paris Universal Exhibition of 1900.

Tony Grubhofer: the British Pavilion at the Paris Universal Exhibition 1900.

Goncourt, who was entranced not only by the beauty of the flowers when they came into bloom, but also by their exotic titles; *Cloud of Bronze, Bamboo under Snow,* and *Scent of Women's Sleeves.*

Hayashi was an able dealer and quite conversant with all the tricks which can be used to excite the greed of a collector. He made a point of being extremely secretive, of making it as difficult as possible for clients to see what he had in stock, thus making them more eager to purchase as they became convinced that he had a particular choice treasure which would be snapped up by a rival collector. Versed as he was in the ways of collectors, he underestimated the guile of a really determined connoisseur.

Hayashi had a mistress, a French girl with whom he lived very happily. In 1889 he went on a long trip to the Orient and was away for over a year, buying not only for himself but for Bing and various other dealers, having arranged to send curiosities back to his mistress who would arrange for them to be shown to the various dealers in Paris. After his departure she began to receive the ardent attentions of a certain Gillot, a printer who was also a collector of Japanese art—attentions which she found impossible to resist. Very soon Bing and the others noticed that the objects which Hayashi was sending back were not only few in number but also poor in quality. Gillot, more interested in Japanese art than in Hayashi's mistress, had profited from her infidelity to obtain the best pieces for himself.

Tadamara Hayashi, like most of the Japanese dealers in Paris, was acquainted with most of the artists and designers of the day, who if not able to be collectors often visited his shop to inspect his stock. Among them was the typographer Georges Auriol, whose designs for type-faces were still being used on the covers of Larousse in the 1930s. Auriol designed monograms for his friends and the popularity of these led to his being commissioned to compose trade marks for commercial firms, some of which were published in *Le Livre des Monogrammes, Marques et Cachets* in 1892, followed by a second volume seven years later. The illustrations, nearly a thousand in number, are completely different from the conventional monograms of intricately enlaced and often indecipherable initials which were embroidered on linen or cut into seals. With a wit and a directness obviously derived from Japanese family crests, he contrived to incorporate initials in a script inspired by Persian writing and Japanese grass charac-

ters, and sometimes an emblem in an area often no more than a half-inch in diameter, the subjects ranging from a personal monogram for Madame Cheruit, the most elegant dressmaker in Paris, to a commercial commission for Cadbury's chocolate which was still in use until a recent date. His device for Hayashi combined the silhouette of Mount Fuji-

yama and a temple gateway ingeniously formed from Hayashi's initials.

In 1892, Hayashi made another prolonged trip to America and the Far East, a trip which lasted two years and during which, for part of the time, he was accompanied by Bing. The length of this journey was probably due to the difficulty they experienced in finding good speci-

mens of Japanese art, for owing to developments in Japan there had arisen a class of *nouveau riches* who were anxious to buy antiquities which would give them a certain prestige, and who were forcing up the prices. While on this trip, Hayashi was instrumental in bringing to the notice of the Japanese Government the important rôle de Goncourt had played in developing an appreciation of Japanese art in France, and he was able on his return to Paris to hint to de Goncourt that it was possible that he would be honoured by a decoration from the Japanese Government.

This did much to mollify the ageing de Goncourt who, morose at the best of times, was now ill. For many years he had been, like so many Frenchmen, obsessed by anti-semitism, and this had shown itself already in his relations with Bing who was, into the bargain, a German — another reason for detestation.

Tadamara Hayashi, who as a fellow dealer had every reason for not wanting to offend Bing, had added fuel to the growing fire by excusing himself from giving any more information to de Goncourt for his book on Hokusaï on the grounds that Bing was also preparing a volume on the same subject, and he felt that he could not afford to get on the wrong side of a colleague with whom he had so many ties of business and friendship. De Goncourt exploded in fury, reminding Hayashi of the large sums of money he had spent in his shop and that he was entitled to the consideration due to a good client. Hayashi, he pointed out, had no cause for complaint — he may have helped de Goncourt with a previous book on the subject of Utamaro but his time and trouble had been recompensed by de Goncourt with a payment of three hundred francs out of the twelve hundred payment for the book. As de Goncourt had borrowed a large collection of prints from Bing and had asked Hayashi to translate the inscriptions on them, and to explain the significance of various details before they were returned to Bing, it may well be that the latter was quite naturally beginning to feel that de Goncourt was making too much use of him in gathering material for his book without showing any gratitude, and was in addition making unpleasant remarks about him behind his back. It was only natural that under these difficult circumstances he should ask Hayashi to examine his loyalties.

The storm finally burst in 1896. Two months previously Bing had opened his new venture, 'L'Art Nouveau', and the ailing de Goncourt — he died in the following July — savagely criticised the opening exhibition, recording his opinions in his journal. It is safe to assume that his remarks in conversation were no less vitriolic and that Bing was soon made aware by mutual friends of de Goncourt's feelings about him. Bing seized the opportunity in February 1896 of pointing out in an article in *La Revue Blanche* that a considerable part of de Goncourt's forthcoming life of Hokusaï was a plagiarism of a biography which Bing had commissioned from a Japanese writer. As the accusation was true, de Goncourt's fury was all the greater, and although he tried to minimise the amount of material he had borrowed he had to admit that in the main Bing was correct in his accusation. The editors of *La Revue Blanche*, most of whom were Jewish, and the unfortunate Hayashi, who had been concerned in the translation of the original Japanese book, were all denounced by de Goncourt.

The following April de Goncourt was obliged to visit 'L'Art Nouveau' for the private view of some paintings by an old friend, Eugène Carrière. Unavoidably he met Bing who greeted him, much to de Goncourt's disgust, as though nothing had happened and made an attempt at a reconciliation by asking de Goncourt to participate in an exhibition of modern books to be held at 'L'Art Nouveau' by lending some of his bookbindings, and in particular his unique collection of books chosen by his author friends as being their best work and bound in white vellum, upon which artists of their choice had either drawn their portraits or decorated with designs. This collection was de Goncourt's pride, and instead of being delighted that it should be considered worthy of being the centrepiece of an exhibition of modern craftsmanship, he refused to accept the olive branch, shook off the hand Bing had placed on his arm and left. The two men never saw each other again, and after de Goncourt's death, when according to his wishes his collections of eighteenth-century French furniture, paintings, drawings, books and manuscripts, as well as those of Oriental art, should be sold for the benefit of other collectors and not 'buried in museums, where they would be exposed to the vulgar gaze of indifferent passers-by', it was Bing who was called in as an expert to catalogue the Far Eastern collection which was sold by auction in March 1897, realising the sum of a quarter of a million francs.

De Goncourt's prejudice against Bing's essay in what was at the time considered to be *avant-garde* is easy to understand, for even if it had not been the work of someone who was the object of his personal antagonism, it is doubtful if it would have met with his approval. All his life he had steeped himself in the traditions of the eighteenth century, and his enthusiasm had awakened a revival of interest in the furniture and decoration of the *Louis Quinze* and *Louis Seize* periods. Together with his brother Jules whose death had been such a crushing blow and had condemned him to years of spiritual loneliness, he had made an intensive study of the manners and personalities of the eighteenth century, had come to know them as though they were living people and had made them come alive for others. He had found solace for his grief in discovering the beauties of Japanese art, though there was always the regret that Jules was not there to share his discoveries. Alone he had formed one of the finest collections of the art of the Far East, but he failed to realise the source of inspiration which Japanese art was proving to contemporary artists. The new art was to his bitter and inflexible mind an insult to all he prized and esteemed.

'*l' Art Nouveau*'

'*L'Art Nouveau qui est l'image fidèle de l'époque
indécise et vague que nous traversons.*'

For some years, approximately from 1890 onwards, Bing in
company with other dealers in Japanese art had been finding it
increasingly difficult to keep up the high standard of merchandise which had become associated with his establishment. The
Japanese were grateful to French dealers and collectors for
spreading information of the beauty of their artistic culture to
the Western world and for making known in Europe that they
were not ignorant and barbaric 'Annamites', but the increasing knowledge of Japanese culture was also making those
same dealers and connoisseurs more demanding in their
requirements. The novelty of Japanese art had worn off in the
thirty-five years since it first began to appear in Europe, but
the demand had increased and instead of being enthralled by
anything Japanese, no matter how indifferent, serious collectors had realised that the Japanese art which was being sent
over was mainly contemporary. They were beginning to
demand the more precious, older examples, and the fear arose
in Japan that the artistic heritage of the country would soon

disappear into the collections of France, England and America. A new class of recently rich people was rising in Japan, people who, as is always the case, were anxious to give themselves some semblance of prestige and tradition by forming collections of works of art and these people were forcing up the prices to such an extent that Bing, Sichel and Hayashi were finding their buying trips to Japan increasingly fruitless. Bing must have been aware of the growing interest in bringing together the fine and the decorative arts and that so many of the decorative objects being produced by artists and craftsmen of his acquaintance were obviously influenced by Japanese art; obviously, these objects would harmonise with his diminishing stock of oriental works of art. For some years previously he had been holding exhibitions of contemporary artists and the success of these influenced his decision to open a gallery entirely devoted to a permanent display of modern decorative art in conjunction with exhibitions of paintings. It would be housed in an eighteenth-century building at the corner of the Rue de Provence and the Rue Chauchat, probably next door to the shop which de Goncourt had visited for the first time twenty years earlier. The scheme necessitated the transformation of the interior and the exterior of the building and this task was entrusted to the architect Louis Bonnier.

When the time came to plan the decorations for the new venture, which included the complete transformation of an eighteenth-century house into a shop and galleries in the new style, his choice of artists to carry out mural paintings was interesting.

Of all the arts, painting was the one least affected by Art Nouveau. While Hector Gulmard was pre-eminent in architecture, Emil Gallé in the creation of glassware, René Lalique in jewellery, Alphonse Mucha and Jules Chéret in poster design, there is no name among the contemporary French painters which springs to mind as being the 'Art Nouveau' painter. The reasons for this are complex. The idea, general in the seventeenth, eighteenth and the first decades of the nineteenth century, that the decoration of a room, its furniture and ornaments, should be combined in a harmonious whole, had been lost sight of in the general welter of vulgarity which was prevalent during the middle of the century, when a room was not considered to be fashionable unless it was overcrowded with furniture in a pastiche of different period styles, and the walls covered with an assortment of paintings of various subjects which had only the heaviness of their gold frames in common, and which were interspersed with porcelain plaques, brackets supporting sculpture, and collections of weapons. The close relationship which had existed between the patron and the painter during preceding centuries had tended to disappear with the rise of the picture dealer, who not only acted as a middleman but also tended to act as a barrier between them, in that a painter whose work was sold in a gallery not only had no idea where the painting was to hang, but probably never saw it again. Portraits were of necessity an exception. The artist began increasingly to regard his paintings as expressions of his own personality and emotions, that when they were finished they could be sold as merchandise. The increasing number of artists, and the proliferation of exhibitions—it was not uncommon for a mixed exhibition to number the works shown in thousands—made competition among artists extremely keen.

In general, painting and the decorative arts bore little relationship to each other. The École des Beaux Arts was primarily intended to teach drawing, painting and sculpture, according to the classic principles, and other branches of the arts were considered negligible (the fees for tuition were much less for them than for the fine arts) while other studios, such as the Académie Julien, were restricted to the teaching of painting, and students were given no encouragement to take an interest in other forms of creative expression. Well-established artists would have a number of pupils who would be taught only drawing and painting. Attempts were made during the closing decade of the century to close the gap by including in the big annual exhibitions a section devoted to decorative arts where furniture, glass, metalwork, including jewellery, pottery, and even on one occasion an elaborately embroidered dress, could be exhibited alongside paintings. Efforts had been made to bridge the gap as early as 1864 with the creation of the Union Centrale des Beaux Arts appliques à l'Industrie.

In 1876 the substantial sum of 300,000 francs was granted to found schools of design in the French provinces and three years later, in 1879, 350,000 francs were assigned for the establishment of schools of industrial design. This initiative was not, however, maintained and by the late 1890s there no longer existed an organisation for the teaching of industrial design to apprentices in industry. Public opinion, led by enlightened minds and voiced in the press, led to the inclusion in the Salon de la Société Nationale of 1890 of a section devoted to the decorative arts — an example followed by the Société des Artists Français. From that date most of the big annual exhibitions included a section devoted to the contemporary furniture, glass, metalwork, pottery and even on one occasion an elaborately embroidered dress. With few exceptions, painters — even those specialising in decorative painting — tended to ignore the new movement and were not attracted by the ideals of the designers.

Bing, therefore, had to find painters whose work would harmonise with the objects he proposed to exhibit, so that his purpose in furthering the principles of art applied to the surroundings of daily life could be advanced. Albert Besnard was already celebrated, the light fresh colourings of his paintings would enhance the objects displayed and his fame would attract attention to the new venture. Georges de Feure was beginning to be noticed as a decorative artist and his work had a strange dreamlike quality which would not be out of place. Frank Brangwyn had worked with William Morris and Burne-Jones. Morris chintzes had been on sale at Bing's shop and elsewhere in Paris for some years and were popular, (although Burne-Jones was not much admired) but the young painter had obvious talent. Charles Conder was, perhaps, a gamble but the new paintings on silk he was experimenting with had something of the feeling in the poems of Verlaine.

Albert Besnard was twenty-five years old when he was awarded the Prix de Rome in 1874 and thenceforward his career was continuously successful. Rarely has a painter been so loaded with official honours, culminating in his being the first painter to be elected to the Académie Française, and on his death ten years later the first artist to be honoured with a solemn lying-in-state in the courtyard of the Louvre. In 1895 he was at the height of his fame and prestige — his murals at École de Pharmacie attracted most of the young painters of the time on the days when they were on show to the public, although they rapidly deteriorated through the action of sunlight, and the process Besnard had used — and his portraits of Madame Jourdain and Réjane caused him to be inundated with more commissions than he could hope to fulfil. His portrait of his wife, formerly Charlotte Dubray the sculptress, had been on exhibition in nearly every gallery in Europe. Combining the fresh, clear colouring of the Impressionists with academic drawing, he was compared favourably with Delacroix by contemporary artists — Delacroix had come by the 1880s to be regarded as a yardstick by which to measure the talent of a promising painter. His success enabled him to live on the scale of Rubens with a vast studio built to his own design in Paris, and another at Annecy, when the effects of brilliant sunshine falling on snow inspired him when he was executing the paintings for Bing's 'Art Nouveau'. These consisted of a circular ceiling panel and eleven wall panels, which were framed in simple mouldings by Van de Velde, who also designed a mantelpiece for the same gallery. The ceiling represented a circle of eight dancing figures of girls, their long flowing skirts forming swirling arabesques of movement. The wall panels were of Alpine scenes, woods, gorges and glaciers, their dark, rich greens and blues contrasting with the brilliant white, blue and yellow in the ceiling. The woodwork in the room was finished in a deep golden-yellow shade, and the ensemble is said to have had an extraordinary freshness and charm.

Nearly twenty years younger than Albert Besnard, Frank Brangwyn was at the threshold of a brilliant career which was to last nearly sixty years, gain him a title and end in a descending curve from general esteem throughout Europe to near oblivion. Before being commissioned by Bing to collaborate with the architect Bonnier in the conversion of the eighteenth-century house at the corner of the Rue de Provence and the Rue Chauchat, Brangwyn had spent about three years at the William Morris firm in Oxford Street, where he was mainly

occupied in preparing the cartoons for versions in woven tapestry of paintings by Burne-Jones. A period spent at sea had
erased the memory from his mind of the wan, pallid knights
and maidens in sombre and subfusc colours so dear to
Burne-Jones, and his travels in the Orient had left him with
brilliant and vivid impressions, the memories of which, translated into intense colour and boldly modelled forms, formed a
major influence in the development of his highly personal
style—a style which confounded the critics of the day by its
lack of academic finish, its brutal realism and its anti-romantic
approach. In 1895, however, Brangwyn's style was still
undeveloped, although in a short while his characteristic
paintings were to be a feature of practically every exhibition of
paintings throughout Europe and, like Besnard, he was to be
compared with Delacroix and Frans Hals by critics.

Perhaps a more established painter would have baulked at
the task set for the decoration of the exterior of 'L'Art
Nouveau', which consisted of two bands of ornament; one
immediately under the eaves, the other at a lower level, both
running along two sides of the corner building, the total
length being some 180 feet.

According to one contemporary writer, these frescoes were
executed in such a hurry that Brangwyn had no time even to
make preliminary sketches but studies for the final paintings
were reproduced in *The Artist* for 1897, and it was generally
agreed that the paintings were inferior to the drawings. In
justification, it must be said that Brangwyn painted the
frescoes under extremely adverse circumstances, as the weather
was bitterly cold.

The upper frieze was treated in a broad manner with
groups of Oriental figures engaged in various crafts, the bold
outlines in brilliant blue filled in with masses of colour. The
exposed site necessitated all the painting being carried out in
the now-forgotten 'Kiem's Process'—apparently an extremely
arduous method of applying the colours, which should have
rendered them immune to fading and to the effects of the
weather, but it did not do so and the frescoes deteriorated
rapidly in a short time.

The lower band was mainly of foliage interspersed with

figures. Brangwyn's work in the entrance hall consisted of two panels, 'Music' and 'Dancing' executed in very thin washes of oil-colour which gave the effect of a tapestry by leaving the texture of the canvas visible. These panels, more delicate in colour than Brangwyn's usual work, show a strong Japanese feeling in the disposition of the elements which make up the composition, while the figures seem to have been calculated to harmonise with Besnard's floating nymphs. The exterior friezes and these two panels appear to have been the extent of Brangwyn's paintings for Bing, but he executed a number of designs for stained glass windows, carpets and at least one tapestry.

As a result of his trips to America, Bing was conversant with the experimental glass of Louis Comfort Tiffany and for some years was an agent for Tiffany's glass in France. The idea that Tiffany should carry out stained glass windows was a good one but, unhappily, the results were not always as successful as they might have been had Brangwyn been more inclined to acquaint himself with the techniques of stained glass. He disregarded the fact that areas of coloured glass must necessarily be held together by strips of lead which themselves play an important part in the design of the whole, and that the disposition of the emphatic, heavy lines of the leading must be carefully calculated to bring them into a harmonious relationship to the areas of coloured or painted glass. What might have succeeded extremely well if interpreted as a tapestry was often a failure when converted into a stained glass window. In spite of the Tiffany stock of thousands of pieces of coloured glass, the craftsmen often found that the only way to achieve the effect of the Brangwyn designs was to superimpose two—or even three—layers of glass, obtaining in this manner the intensity of colour the artist demanded. The extra thicknesses of these layers formed dust traps, which soon dulled the colours and it was found necessary to enclose the window between two layers of clear plate glass—a very unsatisfactory solution to the problem.

Georges de Feure was the possessor of a fully developed and extremely personal style, and his contributions to Bing's pavilion can be ranked among the finest works in the Art

Nouveau manner. Georges von Feure (the 'von' he afterwards changed to 'de') was born in Paris in 1868, his father a rich and successful architect of Dutch nationality, and his mother Belgian. His parents returned to the Netherlands when he was a baby and his childhood was spent in the security and comfort of a luxurious home. This happy state of affairs was brought to a sudden end when he was barely sixteen, for his father, through a series of unfortunate speculations, was declared bankrupt, the home was sold in an effort to raise as much money as possible, and de Feure was forced to earn his living as best he could, drifting from one job to another, in turn assistant to a bookseller and a hatter before joining a small theatre in Amsterdam where for a pittance he became a general utility man, designing new scenery or posters for the

company, attending to the wardrobe and generally 'filling in' and making himself useful.

On one occasion, the so-called Moorish 'dervish' dancer, who was the main attraction, decided that the fogs of the Netherlands were no substitute for the African sun and decamped without any further warning. Georges de Feure stepped into his shoes, and suitably dressed and painted black performed an impromptu dance that was far more frightening than that of the errant Moor. This contact with the theatre inspired him to attempt to write plays and articles, but this effort at creativity failing he decided to channel his ideas in the direction of drawing and designing. Working in the studio of a firm producing lithographic posters, he soon showed a natural gift for draughtsmanship, combined with a subtle use of colour. By 1890, when he settled in Paris, this young artist was beginning to be noticed, and in the next ten years his output of work in various fields of design was remarkable — textiles, furniture, porcelain, wallpapers, posters, illustrations for magazines and decorative paintings. His posters were eagerly collected, notably that for Loïe Fuller and the beautiful 'Izita' of 1895.

Henri Frantz's comment that Georges de Feure's work was a 'hymn to the beauty of women' was extremely apt, for the artist dedicated his creative talents not only to the portrayal of women but to their surroundings, the rooms, particularly bedrooms and boudoirs, in which they lived and the objects they handled. Like Alphons Mucha, he seems to have regarded women as decorative objects in themselves, rarely depicting them in contemporary costume but always dressed, if dressed at all, in decoratively arranged draperies or in a version of the costume of a romantic and unspecified period of history.

Again, as in the work of Mucha, de Feure is invariably associated with flowers, as in his series of drawings 'Féminiflores', where the symbolic character of the flower is typified by the woman portrayed. The curious parallel with Mucha can be traced further, for in addition to the fact that both artists seem to have developed their 'Art Nouveau' style spontaneously and fully developed, they both had a partiality for similar ranges of colour, for muted greyed pastel tones, avoiding whenever possible hard or brilliant colours, although Mucha in the latter part of his career used more vivid colours on occasion in some posters.

Typical of de Feure's palette was the description of the porcelain he designed for the Limoges firm of Gérard, Dufraissex et Cie in 1900 — the grounds of which were 'a grey green, a reseda green, a grey, a brown of extraordinary delicacy, and a greyish-pink, exquisitely charming in its freshness'.

De Feure's furniture was extremely graceful and elegant and in contrast to the general use of lightly stained wood which framed the elaborately inlaid panels of floral decoration so much in favour with Gallé, Majorelle and others of the Nancy school, de Feure preferred gilding, which was a perfect foil for the delicate tints of the floral damasks and embroidered silks with which he covered his fragile chairs and settees. His rooms were reminiscent of Louis XV boudoirs in their frivolous femininity without the use of any eighteenth-century idioms of ornament. As an alternative to gilding, de Feure used pale woods but combined with unornamental panels veneered in a figured wood, possibly birch or sycamore, which resembled watered silk.

Charles Conder's delicate paintings in gouache and watercolour on silk decorated another gallery. No record of these paintings seems to exist but there are photographs extant of a series of panels acquired for a house in Ladbroke Road,

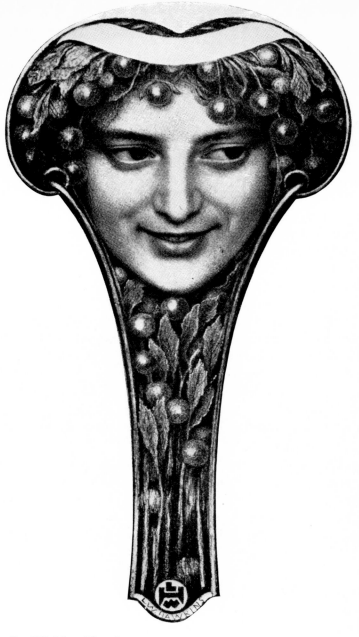

*L. Weldon Hawkins: paper carnival mask. Hawkins,
an English artist working in Paris designed a number
of similar masks some bearing the likeness of
Sarah Bernhardt and other theatrical personalities
and some with trade advertisements.*

Frank Brangwyn: design for a stained glass window.
Commissioned by Bing for 'L'Art Nouveau'.

Frank Brangwyn: carpet designed for 'La Maison Moderne'.
Brangwyn, together with Tiffany and George de Feure
worked for 'La Maison Moderne' the rival firm to Bing's shop.

Charles Conder: panel in water-colours on silk; one of a series of panels set in the satinwood panelling of Mr. Admund Davis's house at Notting Hill Gate, London.

Charles Plumet and Tony Selmersheim: dining room designed for Edouard Detaille, the painter of military scenes.

Alexandre Charpentier: 'La Fuite des Heures'. Clock with a group and bas-relief panels after Charpentier, set in a wooden case designed by Tony Selmersheim. Shown at the third exhibition of 'Les Six at the Galerie des Artistes Modernes', 1899.

Ranavalona III, the deposed queen of Madagascar,
wearing the dress painted with roses by Madeleine Lemaire.
1901.

Notting Hill, by Edmund Davis, and it is possible that these may be the same series of paintings. Unfortunately, the photographs do not include a general view of the room and so the arrangement of the panels is unknown but they seem to have formed part of the panelling and the design of the frames and the small decorative motifs surrounding some of the panels suggest that they are of French rather than English work. If they are not actually the identical panels which were in 'L'Art Nouveau', they are typical of Conder's work and give a good idea of what the panels he did for Bing must have looked like. Lightly painted in luminous washes of opalescent colour on delicately tinted silk, the subjects could be perfect illustrations for Verlaine's 'Fêtes Galantes', at once faintly erotic and yet with an undercurrent of melancholy.

Charles Conder was an Australian who had found his way to Paris where he contrived to study painting. Originally he used the conventional medium of oil-paint but for some reason failed to sell any paintings although they were highly praised. Extremely discouraged by his failure to achieve any recognition, he took to drink and was well on the way to chronic alcoholism when he was persuaded either by Whistler or Sickert to go to Dieppe where there was a small colony of English and French artists. There he soon found himself at the Villa des Orchidées in the care of the Thaulow family, to whom as a matter of course creatures in distress, human or animal, automatically gravitated. Fritz Thaulow, a gigantic Norwegian married to an equally gigantic Russian countess with strong Marxist leanings — it was said the only tune she knew was *The Internationale* — had a large family as blond-pink and white as their parents. He had gained a considerable reputation and a Legion d'Honneur with his large paintings of snow scenes in the Salon of 1889, and his method of working from photographs taken outdoors, which he afterwards worked up in the studio, had at first incurred the deep suspicion of the natives of Dieppe who thought he was spying for the Germans. Conder, a very gauche, lanky figure, always dressed in riding kit although no one had ever seen him anywhere near a horse, was absorbed into this overwhelming family, bursting with health and vitality. Madame Thaulow nursed him back to health by stopping his chain-smoking and forcibly stopped his drinking by putting him on a diet of goat's milk; even his discouragement at his failure to sell his oil-paintings was alleviated when she suggested that he should decorate a silk dress she was wearing with paintings in water-colour. After a few experimental attempts at embellishing the vast expanses of Madame Thaulow, Conder at her husband's suggestion painted some portières which were shown to Bing and led to the commission for the new premises at the Rue de Provence.

The setting for Besnard's paintings was not the only room at 'L'Art Nouveau' designed by van de Velde, who also created a smoking room with panelling and furniture in mahogany, embellished with a large mosaic panel and a painted frieze by G. Lemmen of Brussels. Nothing more alien to French taste could be imagined, and this heavy, cumbersome decoration deservedly aroused the disgust of Edmond de Goncourt, the connoisseur of the finest of French eighteenth-century furniture, to such an extent that he left the building exclaiming to himself 'A frenzy, a frenzy of ugliness' — a remark which was unfortunately taken personally by a young man who was passing by. Originally a painter of the Pointilliste school, van de Velde, like William Morris, was a socialist and became imbued with the idea that painting alone could not serve his ideals of the beautifying of the lives of those less fortunate then himself. Unlike Morris he was, according to a contemporary writer, no abstract idealist fascinated by the Middle Ages and the Renaissance. On the contrary, he loved 'American progress' and did not despise the machine which he saw as a means of reproducing the results of his theories in as great numbers as possible. Ornament or any unnecessary decoration was anathema — the technique, construction and material were enough. This was his doctrine, but it is difficult to see the practical application of his theories to those pieces of furniture or interiors which were photographed and reproduced in contemporary magazines. Constantly in his designs for furniture and panelling the wood is distorted into bizarre curves which betray the nature of the material and which, if they were not so unnecessarily heavy, would result in a structural weakness. Van de Velde's dislike of ornament can be seen in the absence of any carving or relief decoration on his furniture and panelling; he is almost unique among his contemporaries in avoiding any natural forms, floral embellishments or the use of the human figure. The literary element which pervaded the work of Gallé or of Majorelle is not to be found anywhere, and he gained his effects by means of form line and colour. With the aim of imposing unity on the decorations of a room, van de Velde combined various pieces of furniture into a massive unity — a settee surrounded by cupboards and shelves for books or ornaments, the latter often continuing around the room and linking together one or more similar fitments. Van de Velde was credited with this innovation, and in fact used it sparingly, but in spite of criticisms of its impracticability for people living in apartments and the difficulties of adapting these massive constructions on the occasion of a removal to another apartment of a different size, the idea was widely imitated by French decorators — Plumet and Selmersheim, among others.

Van de Velde's work for Bing and for 'La Maison Moderne' does not seem to have aroused a great deal of enthusiasm though his smaller objects, wallpapers and textiles, were more successful, probably because in these he relaxed his theories and was prepared to compromise with commercial demands. His real market he found in Germany, where he founded a shop in Berlin and this, together with a branch in Holland, brought in enough orders to maintain a large factory at Voole, near Brussels. The catalogue of work produced at these workshops ran into six large volumes and included furniture, wallpaper, stained glass, light fittings, book-bindings, jewellery, posters and embroidery, all designed by van de Velde and made under his personal supervision.

Bing's name for his business, 'l'Art Nouveau', was soon adopted in its shortened form of Art Nouveau, as the name of the style he was promoting, according to a contemporary American writer in *The Craftsman*, published in Syracuse, New Jersey. The less explicit title, 'La Maison Moderne', was used by Julius Meier-Graefe when he opened a shop at 82 rue des Petits-Champs in 1898. Three years later 'La Maison

Moderne' published a volume *Documents sur l'Art Industriel au Vingtième Siecle* which stated, in the preface, the aims of the establishment and illustrated with some 270 photographic illustrations of items on sale. The volume was divided into nine sections, each dealing with a separate craft and with an illustrative drawing by Felix Valloton, with typography by Eugene Grasset, a cover design by Paul Follot, and endpapers by G. Lemmen (the designer of the mosaics in the van de Velde smoking room at 'l'Art Nouveau'). The result was a Franco-Belgian co-operative effort.

The anonymous writer of the preface stated that for the previous ten years Meier-Graefe had advocated equality in the arts, endeavouring to convey his passionate conviction, 'qu'il ne soit rien proposé à notre regard, à notre usage que l'Art n'ait ennobli du prestige de la beauté'. The time came when he felt that words were not enough and he took the step of creating 'La Maison Moderne' to pursue the ideals of William Morris, which until 1898 nobody had put into practice in France. Visitors expecting another gallery of paintings and sculpture would be disappointed, but they would find objects which were both beautiful and useful — art applied to everyday objects. Furthermore, the idiom of ornament would be strictly contemporary with no recourse to historicism, for magnificent as the heritage of French art was, it was not applicable either in form or feeling to an age of new discoveries or inventions. For a Frenchman of the twentieth century to live in an apartment decorated in the eighteenth century style was, to a logical point of view, as ridiculous as dressing in a beribboned satin coat and wearing a powdered wig, and even more ridiculous was the use of machine-made adaptations of period ornament to modern inventions — rococo ornaments on an automobile.

The only common characteristic between the furniture of 1901 and that of former epochs should be richness of the materials, harmony of colour and purity of line — there the resemblance should end. Tradition should not be despised but carried on and reviewed. With this aim in view, Meier-Graefe founded a separate studio for each craft, under the supervisioy of an artist whose technical ability was matched by his abilitn as a designer. The façade of 'La Maison Moderne' and the showrooms were designed by van de Velde in his characteristic abstract style with not very happy results, but the majority of the furniture on display was the work of Abel Landry who, according to one writer, had worked with Morris in London. Landry's aim was to provide an almost neutral background, conforming to the rule that his surroundings are made for man, not man for his surroundings, and that they should provide an atmosphere of calm and peace to soothe the nerves 'over-excited by modern life'; Landry's furniture was simple, often elegant, but on the whole undistinguished.

The metal work, which included electric and oil lamps, candlesticks, inkwells and hand mirrors in addition to vases, was, for the most part, mediocre in design apart from the designs of Maurice Dufrêne. The work of a large number of sculptors was shown, including of course a Loïe Fuller by Bernard Hotger, who was the main exhibitor; George Minne also contributed a number of statuettes of emaciated male nudes. The fashion for incised leather, so often used to upholster chairs at this period, was represented by many examples of blotters, picture frames, purses, etc., by Maurice Dufrêne, Paul Follot and others. Most of the porcelain at 'La Maison Moderne' was from the Copenhagen factory of Bing and Grœndhal, but French pottery was represented by works by Dalpayrat, often with metal mounts by Dufrêne, who also designed a considerable quantity of the jewellery shown, while Paul Follot and Manuel Orazzi were also represented by their designs for hair-combs and belt-buckles, both essential elements in the feminine toilette.

'La Maison Moderne' sponsored a revival of the art of handmade lace, which had almost disappeared. The number of Norman lace-makers had declined from 40,000 in 1850 to a few hundred in 1890, and even these few skilled workers could earn barely enough to live on, the taste of the public preferring an antique lace to that made by contemporary workers.

In 1897, Felix Aubert became interested in the craft and designed polychrome lace which was immediately successful. Examples were purchased by museums and in 1898 the

Czarina of Russia was presented by the French Government with a magnificent scarf designed by Aubert. The Empress of Germany acquired from 'La Maison Moderne' an 'evantail aux roses', one of a series of lace fans with a design by Aubert based on different flowers, paeonies, clematis, iris, eglantines, some of which were mounted on tortoiseshell sticks decorated with gold, enamel and precious stones by Maurice Dufrêne. Aubert's polychrome lace was also made into collars and borders. Madame Ory-Robin painted silk fans and parasols, with floral designs in a similar style.

Georges de Feure, whose work for Bing had been so successful, also contributed to 'La Maison Moderne' — his name appears among a list of artists in an advertisement, but nothing of his is illustrated.

A secondary aim of 'La Maison Moderne' was to provide mass-produced objects at a reasonable cost — 'for the last ten, five, two years an object . . . laboriously created by the artist himself remained unique; it was worth its weight in gold. Thanks to mass production, anyone can now buy similar objects at a low price.' Unfortunately, the items illustrated were, for the most part, not particularly distinguished in design and the response of the public to this well-meant venture proved disappointing. The life of 'La Maison Moderne' was short.

An anonymous critic, writing for *The Studio* in 1897, regretted that 'French artists of today seem lost to that feeling of fraternal enthusiasm and are solely concerned with gratifying the ambitions of the moment . . . if only the art workers of real ability and earnest conviction would bind themselves together in a sort of guild, they might then create a national style'.

This observation points one of the great differences between English and French designers; the former banded themselves together into various guilds, taking as their example the mediaeval associations of craftsmen (without going to the length of stipulating standards of craftsmanship, which had to be met before an apprentice could become a fully-fledged member of the guild) and by doing so solved the problem of exhibiting their work — a mass exhibition of handicrafts by all the members of a guild obviously having more impact on the philistine public than one-man shows would have done. The French, on the other hand, were more individualistic, and in any case were able to send their latest works to the newly formed sections of decorative and applied arts of the official exhibitions, the first being that at the Salon du Champs-de-Mars in 1890. One group, however, which approximated the English guilds was 'Les Cinq', whose first exhibition in 1897 was held at the Galerie des Artistes Modernes, which had recently opened in the Rue Caumartin.

The five designers associated were Felix Aubert, already mentioned in connection with 'La Maison Moderne', and working for the firm of Pilon, Huot and Rigotard, specialising in floral brocades and cut velvets; Alexandre Charpentier, well known as a medallist and demonstrating his versatility in sculpture and furniture design; Jean Dampt, a sculptor also designing furniture adorned with decorative sculpture; Henri Nocq, the jeweller, and Charles Plumet, an architect also designing furniture. Later in the year, Selmersheim joined the group, and the name was necessarily changed to 'Les Six'. At the second exhibition of furniture, fabrics and decorative objects by the members of the group, some screens by Plumet incorporated needlework designed by Moreau-Nélaton and executed by Madame Moreau-Nélaton (a victim of the tragic Charity Bazaar fire).

By 1899, when 'Les Six' held their third exhibition, the group had increased to eleven, the new names being Jules Desbois, who exhibited some sculpture in pewter, including a piece named — inevitably — 'Les Libellules'; Mlle Hallé, whose contribution of enamelled jewellery was criticised for the reason that the execution was inferior to the design, and Albert Angst, L. Hérold, and A. Jorrand, whose various contributions of furniture and tapestry aroused little enthusiasm. The quality of the work submitted by the original members of the group was regarded as being of the high standard to be expected from them, but the highest praise was reserved for a clock, the joint effort of Tony Selmersheim and Alexandre Charpentier, which was considered to be equal to any product of the eighteenth century. The case, designed by Selmersheim, was carved in padouk wood, the deep rich violet-crimson colour of which formed a contrast with the three panels in relief, the clock face and the sculptured group, 'La Fuite de l'heure' modelled by Charpentier and cast in gilded bronze with dull-greenish patina. Charpentier's mastery of the art of working in low relief—a mastery which he had demonstrated in the numerous medals and decorative medallions which had made him the celebrated sculptor working in France in this medium—was shown to full advantage in the three panels representing the three Fates, which were inlaid in the base, while the sculptured group surmounting the clock, although possibly a trifle too small in scale, revealed his powers as a sculptor in three dimensions. Time, an elderly, bearded figure in a kneeling position, is trying to prevent the escape of a pair of flying figures—a young man who is embracing a girl, one hand supporting her in the air while the other hand grasps the scythe which he has stolen from Time. The absorption in each other of the two young people is beautifully contrasted with the sorrowful expression of the old man.

The success of this collaboration inspired two other designers, Maurice Dufrêne and the sculptor Voulot to produce a similar clock, which was exhibited at the salon of 1901. Several museums purchased copies, and at the close of the Salon the original model was exhibited at 'La Maison Moderne', where the clock and the sculptural group could, if required, be purchased separately.

This association of artists did not long survive the addition of a number of undistinguished members to the original nucleus, and the group soon dispersed. Charpentier joined the 'Société Novel des Peintres et Sculpteurs' while Plumet and Selmersheim established a successful partnership combining architecture and interior decoration, which lasted for a number of years.

One of the first of the interior decorators—as we understand the term today—was Georges Hœntschel, who wielded a considerable influence in the field of decoration and was unusual in that his enthusiasms embraced both the eighteenth century and Art Nouveau. He worked for a time as a potter in the studio of Carriès and then became a salesman in the firm of Leys which enjoyed the patronage of an extremely rich clientele. He gained a reputation as a connoisseur and as an arbiter of taste. By dint of shrewd buying, combined with a flair for discovering neglected pieces of fine quality, he amassed a collection of eighteenth-century furniture and objets d'art which was only surpassed by that of Jacques Doucet, the couturier. He was responsible for the choice of works and the decorations of the pavilion of the Union Centrale des Arts Décoratifs, where furniture by Abel Landry, Plumet and Selmersheim was shown.

It is impossible to estimate the extent to which the Art Nouveau style was applied to interior decoration, not only in Paris but in the provinces. With the passing of time a great many decorative schemes must have vanished without record in the natural course of events, and how many Art Nouveau interiors still survive more or less in their original form can only be a matter of speculation. Looking through contemporary periodicals, it is tempting to assume that interiors in Paris about 1900 were decorated in nothing but Art Nouveau, but it should be remembered that at the same time there was a revival of the Louis XVI style which owed its origin partly to the influence of the painter Paul Helleu, and more to the work of English firms — Maples, Collinson & Lock, Howard & Sons, to mention only a few. These firms showed furnished rooms at various exhibitions in Paris, and strangely, the white painted furniture in a style with elements of Louis XVI, combined with Hepplewhite, Adam and Sheraton, was extremely popular — and was known irreverently in the trade as 'Louis the Hotel', owing to its wide use in the numerous new hotels which were being built around 1900 in the capitals and resorts of Europe.

For those who could afford it, the pure Louis XVI or Directoire style, using genuine antique furniture, was preferred.

In 1902, Cécile Sorel, the doyenne of the Comédie-Française and famous for her interpretation of the rôle of Celimène in *Le Misanthrope*, installed her collection of jewellery and antique lace in an apartment which was as nearly a copy of the Petit Trianon as was possible, while Yvette Guilbert, the Montmartre singer who had started her career in the shoe department at Printemps built a house in the

Boulevard Berthier, now demolished. The architect Xavier Schoellkopf designed the exterior in a plastic version of Art Nouveau, which resembled the flowing lines of Gaudi's façades. The details, however, were completely Louis Quinze. The supports to the bay window on the first floor incorporated a life-size portrait of the Madamoiselle Guilbert with her eyes fixed on anyone entering the front door. The scrolls surrounding this caprice were in the rococo manner. This decorative theme was carried through in the entrance hall and staircase, but the singer's courage failed when it came to the main rooms which were, like Madame Sorel's, a mixture of Louis Quinze and Louis Seize.

Robert de Montesquiou, the patron of Gallé, and a collector of Japanese art, chose the Louis Seize style for the surroundings, combining furniture of that period with that of the Empire and relegating the Oriental works of art to the corridors and lesser rooms of the house. Although he ordered several pieces of furniture in the Art Nouveau manner from Gallé, his enthusiasm for the style, as far as furniture was concerned, seems to have been short-lived, and was probably an off-shoot of his greater enthusiasm for Japanese art.

The controversy which surrounded Art Nouveau and the violence of the opinions either for or against it — mostly the latter — must have proved a deterrent to anyone contemplating a redecoration in the new manner. Another factor was that it was undoubtedly expensive owing to its needing to be made by hand if the full beauty and significance of the original designs were to be realised in the finished piece of furniture or panelling. After the 1900 Exhibition, when the style was commercialised, the standard of workmanship tends to degenerate with the introduction of machine-made components, the result being that Art Nouveau became less interesting to a discriminating purchaser. Also the large number of restaurants and cafés which were redecorated in Art Nouveau (a phenomenon comparable to Miss Cranston's tea rooms in Glasgow and the Kardomah Arts and Crafts teashops in England) and, in particular, the dubious reputation of Maxim's, which was redecorated in the new manner, may have added to the prejudice which was already existing.

'La Maison de l'Art Nouveau'

The theme of Bing's pavilion was stated in the exterior decorations of the low, one-storeyed building by de Feure. The name of the architect, if any, is not recorded. Decorative painting of 'Architecture', 'Sculpture' and 'Painting' depicting elegant Parisiennes symbolically posing in suitable attitudes flanked the entrance, giving the pavilion a curious resemblance to the exterior of the portable theatre painted for La Goulue by Toulouse-Lautrec. The cornice consisted of a band of an orchid motif, many times larger than life and in high relief, which provided an indication of the exoticisms of the interior. The vestibule, designed by Gaillard, was decorated with pink draped walls below an elaborately stencilled frieze, and was furnished solely by a large armoire of walnut and mirror. The floor was of mosaic. Walnut was the main wood used in the dining room, also by Gaillard, and the least successful of the rooms. The walls were panelled to a third of their height in walnut with contriving decoration at the height of a chair back of abstract scrolls in bronze. The rest of the walls were covered with Sert's paintings in shades of grey and yellow.

Sert, whose full name was José Maria Sert y Badia, was born in 1876 at Barcelona, where his father was a designer of textiles and tapestries. Brought up in an artistic atmosphere, he showed an aptitude at an early age for painting and for mural painting in particular, receiving every encouragement from his parents, who were comparatively wealthy, to travel and in particular to study in Paris. He was thus twenty-four years old when he arrived in Paris in 1900, and was noticed by Bing, who considered his work promising enough to entrust him with the mural paintings in the dining room of the exhibit. Obviously the work of an immature painter, they show the style which was later to bring Sert more commissions than he could execute, and the colour scheme of black, greys and touches of yellow, unusually sombre for the period, is forerunner of the later richer monotone harmonies of brown, gold and silver relieved by accents of vermilion which became his speciality. Some excuse for the deficiencies of the design can be found in the fact that the paintings must have been conceived and executed in a very short space of time for the interval between Sert's arrival in Paris and the opening of the Exhibition was only a matter of, at the most, three months and the inference to be drawn from Bing's giving this important commission to an unknown young painter is that another artist may have let Bing down at the last moment.

Sert's inexperience can also be seen in the over-powering scale of the designs, one panel approximately five feet wide and eight feet high is almost entirely occupied by a gigantic boar, while another panel is monopolised by a larger than life-size bull. A few years after Sert found the opportunities he dreamed of for vast murals, for example those which engaged him for twenty years in the cathedral of Vich, which were destroyed in 1936 in the Spanish Civil War. Sert was, in any case, an odd choice for this exhibit, which was intended to show the finest and most elegant examples of Art Nouveau, for his style of painting was inspired by the Neapolitan decorative painters of the eighteenth century, with reminiscences of Veronese and Tiepolo — a style admirably fitted for the ballets Diaghilev commissioned from him some years later, the entrance hall of a New York skyscraper, or the ballrooms for Philip Sassoon in London and Joshua Cosden in Palm Beach, where Sert came under the hypnotic spell of that wayward genius, Addison Mizner. The choice of Sert by Bing, possibly as a last resort, gives an idea of the difficulty of finding a talented painter working in the Art Nouveau manner.

A dining table, a set of single and arm chairs covered in embossed leather, and a large cabinet, all in walnut with bronze applied ornaments en suite with the panelling, completed the furnishing of the room. The enormous skylight of glass was ornamented with scrolls which echoed the more elaborate design of the carpet, also designed by Gaillard. The cabinet, a very handsome piece of furniture, had two glass doors and open shelves in the upper part, which displayed for the Exhibition porcelain and glass, the latter probably by Tiffany, while the lower part was enclosed by four doors carved in relief with typical whiplash scrolls. The salon, which one entered on leaving the dining room, was designed by Colonna in a colour scheme of green and yellow. The walls were covered in a velvet in dull green, the curtains and chair coverings in green and yellow, the pale golden satinwood furniture lightly carved with scrolls, and the tops of the tables and the panels of several cabinets inlaid with formal designs reminiscent of floral forms. A display cabinet held numerous pieces of iridescent gold and green Tiffany glass. Georges de Feure's boudoir, the next room, was described as resembling a 'field of flowers under the moonlight', an effect arrived at by the colour scheme of grey-blue, grey-mauve and grey-green. The walls were panelled in a floral brocade and the delicate gilt furniture was covered in silk embroidered with motifs which elaborated and complimented the design on the walls. Connected to the boudoir by a passage lit with stained-glass windows by de Feure was the dressing room, again panelled in a floral brocade. Here de Feure used ash for the furniture, consisting of a dressing table, cupboards, a wash-stand, a chaise longue and single chairs, which were covered in a plain heavy silk embroidered with motifs of roses.

Bing's pavilion was only half finished at the opening of the Exhibition, and was barely completed before it closed, and it is easy to see that such an elaborate project could encounter difficulties in completion to a time-limit. All the furniture was specially made with carving that could only be done by hand, the silks of the wall coverings and for upholstering the furniture specially woven in intricate designs, while other chairs and settees were decorated with embroideries which could only be done by the most skilful workers. It would be interesting to know the cost of the whole exhibit, which must have totalled a considerable sum of money, and to discover what happened to these exhibits — the Gaillard dining room chairs and a piece of furniture in the same style as the large piece of furniture in the dining room appear in a photograph of a room at Hamburg Museum, which was reproduced in *Kunstgewerbeblatt* for 1902. According to *L'Art Decoratif* de Feure's exhibit attracted so much attention that Bing installed an improved version in his premises at 22 rue de Provence.

Unquestionably, Bing's 'Maison de l'Art Nouveau' was one of, if not the, finest ensembles in the style and it received more publicity than any other example of contemporary decoration in the entire exhibition. It was Bing's swan song. None of the designers, with the exception of Sert, was to achieve anything of comparable importance.

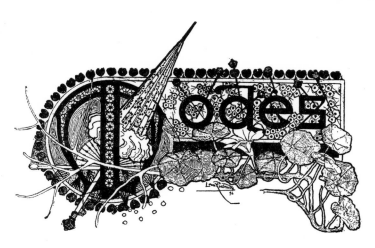

'Luxe, Calme, et Volupté'

The designers of the Art Nouveau were almost without exception preoccupied with femininity and the objects they designed were invariably created for use by women in boudoirs and salons. Georges de Feure is recorded as having said

that he designed with only women in mind and when he started a school of design he would only accept female students. Art Nouveau, like the Louis Quinze style, was essentially feminine in character. In view of this it is surprising to find that women's fashions were barely affected by the style. The descriptions of advance fashions in French magazines such as *Femina* make no acknowledgment of the revolution in other fields of design apart from an indication of an Art Nouveau belt, buckle or piece of jewellery. Even lace, so much a part of the contemporary fashion, was for the most part made in traditional patterns although there were pioneers like Madame Ory-Robin and Felix Aubert who exhibited Art Nouveau lace fans, collars and parasols. Henri van de Velde's efforts to integrate women's fashions in the new style met with little enthusiasm and photographs of his wife in the dresses he designed for her explain this lack of response, for the unfortunate lady seems to be more upholstered than dressed and it is understandable that a chic Parisienne would not willingly resemble a perambulating settee. She might willingly submit to the tyranny of her corsetière — one actress was so tightly laced from her armpits to her knees that she was never able to sit down on the stage and it was written into her contract that she should never be required to take a rôle that entailed her doing so — but Art Nouveau was never allowed to invade her

person — except in the guise of jewellery. Paris would never follow the example of Berlin, where in 1886 a movement had started to originate a new national costume, mainly for women, and a 'reform dress' had been launched. In spite of the considerable sensation that this caused, it was not for another twelve years that designers interested themselves in the idea to any great extent and in 1898 competitions were organised in various towns throughout Germany. The prizewinning designs were exhibited in Berlin together with some ideas by van de Velde and Peter Behrens. From this emerged the 'New Reform Dress' which enjoyed a brief fashion. No corsets were worn under the Princess type dress which hung from the shoulders with no indication of a waist-line, the neck-line was modestly high while the long, rather full sleeves were gathered into a band at the wrists. The effect was extremely Wagnerian and every un-Parisian — which was probably the intention. A fête was organised by the German Society for the Improvement of Women's Dress which was attended by hundreds of ladies mostly in the new dress, though a frivolous minority

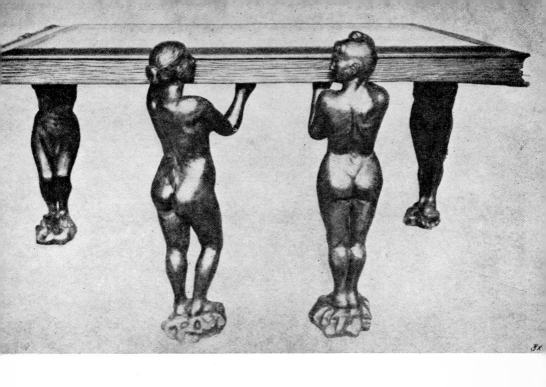

François Rupert Carabin: *library tables and chair.*

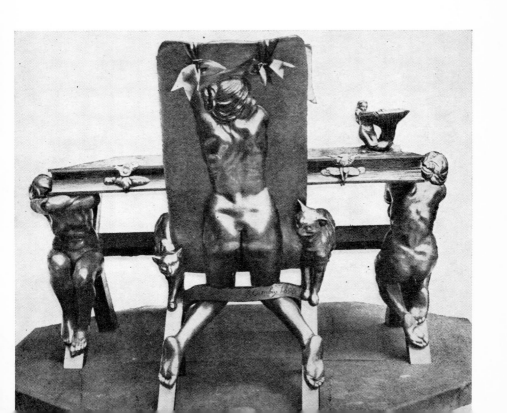

'*Le Palais Lumineux*': *according to the official guide to the Exhibition the Palais Lumineux was constructed entirely of glass made by the Glaceries de Saint-Gobain and the Verreries de Saint-Denis (Legras). Lit by some twelve hundred electric maps this enchanting fantasy which combined the styles of Pillement and Meliès was a setting for a large terrestial globe supported by the figure of a sleeping Red Indian. Demonstrations of glass blowing were given in the basement and glass souvenirs could be bought.*

*Victor Prouvé: evening dress with embroideries
executed by Courtex. Exhibited at the Salon de
La Sociéte Nationale des Beaux Arts — the first time
a dress was shown at an exhibition with the idea
of its being considered as a work of art.*

*Henri van de Velde: the façade of 'La Maison Moderne' opened in
1898 at 82 Rue des Petits-Champs, Paris.*

*Abel Landry: dining room furniture ornamented with
pewter panels designed for 'La Maison Moderne'.*

The entrance to 'Art Nouveau' Bing's exhibit in the 1900 Exhibition. The decorative panels by Georges de Feure are surmounted by a frieze of orchids in high relief.

Georges de Feure: 'La Porcelaine', decorative panel for the exterior of 'Art Nouveau'.

Louise Abbéma: portrait of the novelist GYP (the Comtesse de Martel) in her Japanese studio at Neuilly. 1902.

'*L'Evantail Madeleine Lemaire*': *Mesdames
Blumenthal, Brun and Trousseau attending a
fancy dress ball given by Madeleine Lemaire
in 1901.*

appeared in more conventional and prettier dresses. Dancing was solemnly organised to show the superiority in movement of the reformed dress. However, it was admitted that not all the dresses were successful and nothing more was heard of the Reform Dress.

There was, however, an occasion in Paris when the visitors to the private view of the Societé Nationale des Beaux-Arts in 1901 were surprised to see for the first and only time a dress among the exhibits of painting and sculpture. Such a frivolous break with tradition was justified on the grounds that the design by Victor Prouvé, a collaborator of Emil Gallé, and the embroidery by Courtex were of such exceptional quality as to raise the robe to the level of a work of art. Simply cut, it was of cream silk decorated with the theme of the bank of a river in springtime, a deep band of silver Cluny lace embroidered in undulating lines to represent water out of which water-lilies, iris and other aquatic plants rose almost to the waist. The bodice was heavily decorated with flowers and a large dragon-fly brooch in gold and enamel. Silver water-lilies at the shoulders held up strings of pearls and the long Watteau train of silk muslin was ornamented with silver sequins and more dragon-flies. It was said that the Empress of Germany had expressed a wish to see this creation but no hopes of her buying it were

entertained as she was noted for her economy where dresses were concerned.

It is easy to see that a piece of jewellery — comparatively small and delicate in workmanship — could give an artist working in the Art Nouveau style opportunities for freedom of expression denied in other fields of design, and that having created a work in which he had given full rein to his sense of fantasy he stood a good chance of finding a market for it if it were of sufficiently high standard. A fashionable woman could acquire a piece of jewellery in the contemporary fashion — thus showing her awareness of current trends and at the same time adorning herself — but to undertake to redecorate her salon or her boudoir in Art Nouveau would not only involve her in a lengthy and expensive process but in doing so she took the risk of exposing herself to the unkind comments and even ridicule of her less fashion-conscious friends — just as Saint-Loup found himself derided by Madame de Guermantes when he exchanged his Boulle furniture and family heirlooms for furniture from Bing's 'Maison de l'Art Nouveau'. Even the purchase of a single piece of Art Nouveau furniture might present the problems of its not harmonising with the rest of her furniture. But any woman with pretensions to elegance could safely risk her reputation for taste by indulging herself in the purchase of a piece of contemporary jewellery whether it be a belt buckle by Paul Follot or by Boutet de Monval or a comb by René Lalique.

The women's magazines of the period regularly featured articles on the latest ideas in jewellery and gave prospective readers taking a year's subscription the opportunity of obtaining — at a considerably reduced price — a piece of Art Nouveau jewellery designed especially for the magazine by Lucien Gaillard, or by Beaudoin, and on one occasion a comb designed by Gaillard was given as a prize in a  competition to choose from a number of European princesses a suitable bride for the Crown Prince of Germany.

The fashionable women of the Third Republic, that is to say from 1870 onwards, had not been particularly interested in questions of design or workmanship when choosing a piece of jewellery — their main concern was that it should glitter as much as possible, and if not set with real diamonds the paste would do. In 1867, immediately prior to the troubles of the Franco-Prussian War which led to the disaster of Sedan and the occupation of Paris by the Prussian army, the jeweller

Massin, reacting against the mode for jewellery either from or inspired by that of the Italian Renaissance, or examples found in Etruscan tombs, had succeeded in setting a fashion for jewels in the shape of flowers, bows of ribbon and feathers executed entirely in diamonds, and often with parts of the jewel on small springs so that it trembled with the movements of the wearer, thus accentuating the sparkling effects of the gems. For a quarter of a century this type of ornament remained in fashion, and continued to do so with grandes cocottes who were less concerned with design than with diamonds. But in 1893 attention was drawn to a new and revolutionary designer who was to become the finest jeweller of the Art Nouveau period and may well be ranked among the greatest of any period. René Lalique was thirty years old when he

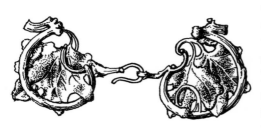

exhibited at the Societé des Artistes Français the jewellery he had designed for Sarah Bernhardt, and his career had been varied since his apprenticeship to the jeweller Louis Aucoc in 1876, including two years studying at an art school in England and the management of the Destape workshops. Having made an intensive study of Egyptian, Byzantine and Florentine jewellery, and also of Japanese metal work, he realised that semi-precious stones and materials such as ivory and even glass combined with enamel were more suited to the current tends in decorative art than the white hard glitter of the diamond, a stone which he used only as an accent or as a foil for a colourful, opaque stone. Although limited by the forms of pieces of jewellery in fashion — brooches of various sizes, hair combs, pendants, plaques for dog-collars of seed pearls, belt clasps and accessories such as lorgnettes — rings and earrings were out of favour and bracelets were not revived until 1904 — he showed an extraordinary fertility of invention combined with a consummate craftsmanship. His polychrome ornaments were immediately popular — jewels were once more raised to the level of works of art rather than displays of wealth — not that Lalique's creations were anything but costly, in spite of his use on occasion of such inexpensive materials as glass or horn, for the workmanship was always of the highest quality.

Gold itself was treated so that it became green or pink according to the needs of the design. Lalique introduced the use of horn of a soft honey-colour which was carved with exquisite skill to make hair combs representing flowers, autumn leaves or the seed pods of sycamore, often with the details accentuated in gold or silver or with tiny gold insects.

Artists were obsessed to the point of fetishism with women's hair, which seems to have, as they depicted it, a separate life of its own, not agitated by the wind but curling in arabesques like the tendrils of a plant seeking to entwine itself around a support or a victim. Not since the drawings of Fuseli had so much attention been paid to women's hair as a decora-

tive motif, and this absorption extended to literature. For instance, in Pierre Louys' erotic novel *Aphrodite*, even on the first page there is a lyrical description of the golden tresses, 'cette toison précieuse', which gave the name of Chrysis to the heroine, and one of the three fatal gifts which she exacted as a price of her favours from the hero Demetrios, and which led to her death, was a comb.

No less than ten combs of blond horn decorated with gold, pearls or diamonds, were among the jewellery sold in 1902 among the effects of Wanda de Boncza who was described as 'Une délicieuse actrice, une des reines de l'élégance moderne'. Her collection of jewellery, partly antique and partly in the Art Nouveau style, included her famous necklaces, one of forty-three matched pearls with a diamond solitaire clasp, another of 1,600 pearls with an Art Nouveau centre ornament of diamonds and translucent enamel, thirty-six rings, twenty-one brooches, but only two pairs of earrings — which had gone out of fashion — but one pair was of enormous, perfectly-matched white pearls, while the other was of black pearls.

There can be no doubt that Lalique was influenced by the glass of Emile Gallé, who had been exhibiting regularly in Paris for some years before Lalique's début as a designer, and it is significant that Lalique eventually abandoned designing jewellery and concentrated on designing and making glass. Like Gallé, his motifs were drawn from flowers and insects, in particular the dragonfly which had as much attraction for him as for other designers of the period. He created this fragile insect either semi-naturalistically or transformed it into a mythological hybrid with the head or the body of a woman. But unlike Gallé, who had abandoned the use of the human figure as a decorative motif very early in his career, he had a partiality for using a plaque carved of ivory or glass with one or more female nude figures as the centrepiece of a design. In view of the beauty of Lalique's jewels, it is surprising to find contemporary criticisms of his work lacking in style and having an 'unhealthy complexity'.

Lalique's lesson that jewellery could be a medium of ideas in design had the unfortunate effect that designers less restrained than he began to indulge in the bizarre and the eccen-

tric which soon brought about a reaction against the style. By
1902 Gabriel Mourey was commenting in *The Studio* that
the bad imitations of Lalique's work almost made one hate the
work of the master and it was probably this that led Lalique to
abandon the designing of jewellery and to concentrate on
working in glass. Lalique's annoyance at the inept versions of
his latest creations made him cautious about exhibiting his
work and he re-
fused to allow an
interviewer from
the English maga-
zine, *The Artist*, to
inspect his recent
work for fear of
plagiarism.

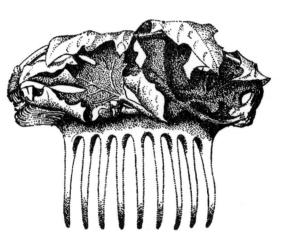

These imitators
suffered, however,
from the dis-
advantage of
having limited
means at their
disposal as well as limited knowledge of the techniques of
jewellery manufacture. Lalique's success at an early stage in
his career, and the recognition among connoisseurs of a
new and exciting talent, had deservedly brought him a number
of commissions from extremely rich patrons, and he was thus
able to exercise his imagination unfettered by any considera-
tions of cost. The financial rewards from his jewellery had
enabled him to build a combined house and workshop in the
Cours-la-Reine which he occupied from 1902. As was so
often the case the Art Nouveau decoration was an encrustation
on a building which the architect had modelled too closely,
according to critics, upon Renaissance forms but the characteristic touch of Lalique could be seen in the wrought iron
decorations of pine trees and cones. The interior, which
included a large exhibition hall for the display of jewellery
and glass, was further decorated with the same motifs and
with glass panels of nude athletes in relief—similar to one to
be seen in the foyer of Claridge's Hotel in Brook Street.

He could build a jewel around a magnificent specimen stone, using it as a centre piece and enhancing it with elaborate and costly workmanship in gold and enamel. In common with the other professional jewellers, Vever and Fouquet, for example, he had been trained to think primarily in terms of metal and precious stones and knew the affinities between certain gems and how to display them to their best advantage. Designers such as Eugene Grasset, lacking this professional training, talented though they may have been in their own field of furniture design or the graphic arts, produced drawings which necessarily had to be interpreted by working jewellers who may have done their best to translate a two-dimensional design into a three-dimensional object, but lacked the supervision of one as versed as themselves in the techniques — who 'spoke the same language'.

A contributory factor in the success or failure of a design was, as always, the temperament and personality of the individual commissioning the jewel, and a good example of this can be seen by comparing the jewellery by Colonna for Bing with that by the same designer for Meier-Graefe's 'Maison Moderne', which was less extravagant, mediocre and undistinguished. Bing, a man steeped in the exotic art of Japan and accustomed to luxurious surroundings, inspired Colonna, while Meier-Graefe's more puritanical leanings, combined with his fervour for the more socialistic themes of William Morris, seem to have had a debilitating effect on Colonna.

The question of finance also had to be taken into consideration. Presumably the jewellery which was on sale at shops like 'L'Art Nouveau', 'La Maison Moderne' and others, was either commissioned by the owners of the shops who hoped that the reputation of the designers would encourage people to buy their creations, or it was paid for by the artist himself and submitted to the shop on sale or return. In either case, the amount of money invested would be limited in the one case by the amount of faith the owner of the shop had in the talent of the artist, and in the other by the means at the disposal of the designer. Any jewels left unsold could only be disposed of by breaking up and realising as much as possible on the raw materials — the gold or silver, and selling the metal and stones — the cost of the designing and the workmanship being entirely lost. Judging from the comparatively few examples of Art Nouveau jewellery still extant, this must have happened in any case when Art Nouveau went out of fashion, and pieces of jewellery in this style were unsaleable as a result. Certainly much of the silver of the time has subsequently been melted down.

Less inventive but of fine quality was the work of the firm of Vever, which at the time of the Art Nouveau was managed by Paul and Henri Vever, the sons of the founder of the business. No doubt the existence of a substantial clientele who might be alienated by designs too extravagantly following the new fashion deterred Vever from indulging in the fantasies permitted to Lalique, who had made his reputation by breaking with tradition but in comparison Vever's work, although of fine craftsmanship, lacks the invention characteristic of Lalique.

Their realisation of the designs of Eugene Grasset were not always successful, for the effort of translating Grasset's drawings into gold, enamel and precious stones results in a heaviness which narrowly avoids being clumsy. Georges Fouquet, also inheriting a family business, was more fortunate in his association with Alphonse Mucha, who not only designed a number of extremely beautiful pieces such as the chimerical snake bracelet and ring combined for Sarah Bernhardt, but also the decorations for Fouquet's shop in the Rue Royale. Fouquet's style, of all the jewellers of the time, most closely resembled that of Lalique, although on a less bold scale and in general having a more lacey texture through the use of smaller stones. There were of course many other jewellers working, in addition to the three already mentioned, but none of them reached such a high standard of design.

E. Feuillatre specialised in enamelling and had perfected

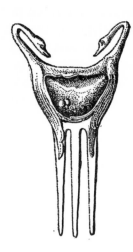

the difficult technique of applying enamel to plantinum; Jules Desbois exhibited a number of handsome gold brooches and buckles, irregular in shape with heads and figures of nymphs in a low relief, giving the impression of having been inspired by early hand-struck Greek coins, although the nymphs portrayed are unmistakably 'fin-de-siecle', and E. Colonna designed jewellery for Bing's 'L'Art Nouveau', which featured baroque pearls set in gold scrolls using the serpentine motifs he incorporated in the furniture for the same firm. He also exhibited some Chinese hardstone snuff-bottles which he had converted into bottles for smelling-salts, and had decorated with silver-gilt ornaments set with precious stones. Boutet de Monval, who had achieved a considerable reputation for his drawings of children, and was later to become a fashionable portrait painter in the United States, was the designer of a number of pieces featuring motifs such as owls and seahorses, and although these were received with enthusiasm he did not continue his experiments in this field. 'La Maison Moderne', established as a rival to Bing's firm, commissioned Paul Follot, Orazzi and Maurice Dufrêne to design a range of ornaments. Orazzi, a poster artist whose affiche for Loïe Fuller in the Japanese manner is a minor masterpiece, was less happy working in metal and his combs and hatpins give a sinister impression with their strange serpent-like forms which crawl over them. Maurice Dufrêne adapted the seaweed motifs he used so often in relief on pewter dishes, vases, and in leatherwork, combining them with enamels and precious stones on cuff-links, umbrella handles and also for mounts for Tiffany glass vases.

Cameo cutting, after a period of neglect, was revived in the closing years of the nineteenth century, particularly by Georges Lemaire, who framed cameos cut in sardonyx in gold frames of his own designing, mostly of flower-entwined scrolls. Henri François, Emile Gaulard and Georges Bissinger created many cameos, some of considerable size, choosing as subjects 'Sappho upon the Rock', 'The Ideal', 'The Messenger of the Gods', featuring pale nudes silhouetted upon a dark layer of sardonyx.

Gloria in Excelsis Cléo
(contemporary witticism)

In 1896 the first beauty competition was held in Paris. This, the ancestor of the 'Miss World' competitions of the present time was organised by Réné Baschet, the editor of *L'Illustration*, and in comparison with its later imitators was an extremely decorous affair. The contestants for the title of 'the most beautiful woman in France' were not required to parade in bathing costumes, to prattle a few banal remarks into a microphone or to reveal their basic measurements to the public. In fact, they did not even attend the competition. Several photographs of each candidate were displayed in the entrance hall of the editorial offices of *L'Illustration* and the public were invited to vote for the one which they considered the supreme beauty of the day.

Sarah Bernhardt, Réjane, Eve Lavallière, Melba, Jane Hading, Baretta, Cécile Sorel, Jeanne Granier, all established stars of the theatre or the opera, were among the twenty-one contestants. Caroline Otéro — 'la belle Otéro' — was an entrant by virtue of her dancing activities rather than her widely publicised career as a demi-mondaine. Seven thousand votes were cast. Over three thousand were in favour of a comparatively obscure dancer from the Paris Opera House who had caused a small sensation by dressing her hair in an individual manner. Beyond a small circle of lovers of the ballet she was unknown to the general public but the three photographs of her which had been displayed were enough for her to run away with the competition. Her name was Cléo de Mérode and overnight she became the most photographed beauty not only during 1896 but for many years to come. Reutlinger, Benque, Auguet and Manuel, the foremost photographers of the time, added considerably to their incomes as the result of the innumerable pictures they took of her, pictures which in postcard form sold by the thousand.

As a matter of interest the winner of the second place was the stately Sybil Sanderson and the improbably named actress Wanda de Boncza, who died five years later at an early age, came third. Otéro was fifth and Sarah Bernhardt sixteenth.

Cléo de Mérode was twenty-one when she became the reigning beauty of Paris. Her parents were Austrian, her father the Baron de Mérode being a member of the Austrian branch of the Belgian family of the same name. Some mystery surrounds the circumstances of her birth in Paris. Her parents had married young, appeared to be ideally happy, united by their love for each other and for a common interest in music and the arts. Just before the birth of her first child, the Baronne was obliged to journey to Paris to settle some legal matters which necessitated her presence. While in Paris a daughter was born to her. She never returned to Austria and seems to have broken off any relationship with her husband whom she never saw again, while he in turn apparently made no effort to follow his wife to Paris or to see his child whom he met for the first time when she sought him out nearly thirty years later when she was internationally famous both as a beauty and as a dancer.

She was christened Diane Cléopâtre, a choice of names which could have proved embarrassing in later life. They were soon shortened to 'Cléo' and she became the admired pet of her mother's growing circle of friends. Knowing nobody when she arrived in Paris the Baronne gradually acquired acquaintances among musical circles. She appears to have been in fairly comfortable circumstances financially and devoted her care and attention to the education of her daughter who was already showing a love and understanding of music.

Thérèse Villard, one of Cléo's playmates at school, had
some aptitude for dancing and her mother succeeded in enroll-
ing the child as a pupil in the ballet school of the Paris Opera.
When Thérèse returned from her classes she would practise
the new steps which had been taught to her in company with
her friend, the seven-year-old Cléo. Noticing that Cléo,
without tuition, was performing the steps as well as if not
better than her daughter, Madame Villard suggested that
Cléo should also apply for enrolment as a pupil. Madame de
Mérode was not enthusiastic about the idea but the pleas of
her daughter overcame her opposition. Cléo in a pleated tartan
dress, a maroon coat and a huge hat decorated with ostrich
feathers — she had a life-long penchant for huge hats decorated

with feathers, some of which can still be seen in museums —
was taken to the Opera House where the child's delicate
beauty, her small neat figure and her obvious grace and
embryonic talent, made an immediate impression and without
any hesitation she was forthwith enrolled as a pupil, to her
great happiness and satisfaction.

Her friend Thérèse seems to have given up any idea of a
career in the ballet but Cléo was undismayed by the hard work
and drudgery of practice classes and her natural aptitude,
combined with that quality of attracting attention which was
to be a lifelong characteristic, soon ensured her being given
small rôles in the opera ballets. At the age of eight she was
dancing minor parts in *Aïda, Faust, Le Cid* and *Thaïs*. When
she was eleven her talents were in demand outside the opera.
The haute-monde were subscribers to the opera more by habit
than from any love of music and their patronage was essential
to the finances of the opera and ballet companies. They were
not a demanding audience and if the standard of dancing was
not high nobody was very much concerned. Male subscribers
expected to be allowed back-stage to mingle with the dancers
of the corps-de-ballet who were for the most part poorly paid
and were only too glad to accept the advances of a protector
who would set them up in a discreet apartment and shield
them from financial adversity. Their wives, well aware of such
situations, either had their own form of distraction or were
busy with their salons where they could take an intimate interest in the careers of young artists, writers or poets. These
salons always had some form of entertainment for the guests
and Cléo de Mérode was much in favour as a dancer on the
nights when she was not engaged in opera performances.

Either alone or partnered by one of her classmates, Berthe
Keller, she performed minuets or gavottes arranged by her
ballet master Monsieur Pluque. As a result of these performances she attracted the attention of several painters including Degas who made a number of sketches of her as did his
friend Forain. In spite of all this flattering notice which had
been taken of her she was still, in the opera, only one of the
humblest members of the involved hierarchy of the ballet
school, beneath the notice of the eminent composers

Saint-Saëns, Gounod, and Massenet in whose work she danced. Massenet, however, had a young pupil of the same age as Cléo de Mérode named Reynaldo Hahn and during the long waits at rehearsals the two children became friends — a friendship which lasted until Hahn's death. One day Reynaldo brought to her mother's apartment one of his friends, a young writer named Marcel Proust, who was rather surprised at Cléo's enthusiasm for Rimbaud, Baudelaire and Verlaine, surprised that a dancer — and a pretty one at that — should have a genuine and informed love of poetry and music. As many others were to do in later years he fell under her spell and became a constant visitor, presenting her with a manuscript *Portrait* which he had dedicated to her — a manuscript which he never allowed to be published and which she treasured until it was stolen during the Occupation.

As time went by she gradually rose in the ranks of the ballet, becoming a 'coryphée' and a year later a 'petit sujet'. At this point in her life she decided that the coiffure which she had worn since childhood was too babyish — a decision which although she could not have known it at the time was to help to make her famous. She allowed her fringe to grow, parted her hair in the middle and drew it down low at each side, completely concealing her ears, and fastened it in a knot at the back of her head. It was not a new or even particularly original style. It was in fact the conventional coiffure of the romantic ballet and when worn with a jewelled ornament hanging on the forehead it became reminiscent of a style recorded by painters of the Italian Renaissance.

Though the current mode was to wear the hair close to the head, it was curled with tongs and back-combed into frizzled pompadours perched above the forehead with often unflattering results, and the simplicity of the 'bandeaux de Cléo', as her hair-style was named, was startling to her contemporaries and was soon copied by others who lacked her perfect oval face with its regular features and large eyes. Liane de Pougy, then at her zenith as a grande cocotte, attempted to wear the hair style adopted by the comparatively unknown ballet dancer but failed to achieve the same effect. Envious rumours began circulating that Cléo de Mérode had adopted her new hair style from necessity, that it was intended to conceal the fact that one ear was deformed: the rumours snowballed until it was common knowledge that both her ears were malformed and even that she had no ears at all. An American newspaper sent a reporter to Europe especially to settle the question once and for all. He visited the dancer in her apartment and sat tongue-tied with embarrassment searching desperately for some way of approaching the subject. Finally Cléo de Mérode who guessed the purpose of his visit took pity on him, and lifting the curtains of hair on either side of her face allowed him to see that they concealed two complete and normal ears. Overjoyed at his coup, the reporter rushed out of the apartment to inform his editor that the American public could breathe again.

Cléo de Mérode had the knack of getting herself talked about and showed a flair for attracting publicity by denying rumours which developed about her through chance circumstances but denying them in such a way that nobody really believed her statements however true they were. Not long after her being acclaimed as the most beautiful woman in France she was approached by the sculptor Falguière who begged her to allow him to model her head. She posed for the sculptor, strictly chaperoned by her mother, but after several sittings he became dissatisfied with his work. He needed to extend the head and wished to add the neck and shoulders to complete the composition. With some reluctance she lowered the neckline of her dress and the work progressed. Having gained this advantage Falguière went on to suggest she should remove her dress as far as the waist so that he might complete the bust. Indignantly she refused but softened her refusal by giving him permission to use a professional model but at the same time insisting that the breasts should be discreetly veiled with a swathe of material. The sittings completed, she heard no more from the sculptor until, to her horror, she was informed that Falguiere was exhibiting at the salon a life-size marble figure entitled 'Danseuse' which had unmistakably her features and coiffeur but which was completely naked. She was immediately besieged by journalists, to whom she naturally denied ever having posed in the nude, calling upon her

George Farcy: drawing room in his own house decorated in shades of rose and green.

George Turck: *library designed for a house at Lille where Turck lived and worked.*

Henri van de Velde: *smoking room designed for 'L'Art Nouveau'. Mahogany with frieze and mosaics by G. Lemmen.*

Theodore Lambert: interior. Lambert was primarily known as a jeweller and his work was often reproduced in 'The Studio'. His volumes on the decorative arts and his designs for interiors and furniture show that he was as versatile as any of his contemporaries.

Mlle. Violette Bichon in the tableau vivant 'L'Art Nouveau à Sèvres' in Act Two of 'Le Carnet du Diable' an operetta presented at the Theatres des Vatietes 1900.

Nadar: photograph of Sada Yacco as La Ghesha in
'La Ghesha et la Chevalier' presented by Loïe Fuller
at her theatre in the 1900 Exhibition.

Cléo de Mérode in the
costume she wore for her
Cambodian dance.

Liane de Pougy wearing a
coiffure copied from that of Cléo
de Mérode. Contemporary
photograph.

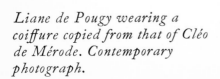

Cléo de Mérode: contemporary photographs.

Elizabeth Wintergerber: design for a house dress.

mother to witness that she was present at all the sittings and could vouch for the truth of her denials. Falguière, on the other hand, equally firmly maintained that she had posed for the entire statue. Nobody knew whom to believe and for weeks Paris talked of nothing else. Crowds flocked to the salon to see the now famous statue and then to the opera to 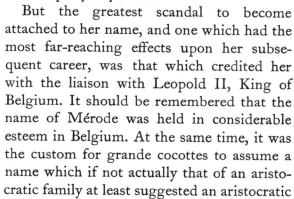 compare it with its supposed original. Both the dancer and the sculptor were adamant in their statements and the publicity did neither party any harm.

But the greatest scandal to become attached to her name, and one which had the most far-reaching effects upon her subsequent career, was that which credited her with the liaison with Leopold II, King of Belgium. It should be remembered that the name of Mérode was held in considerable esteem in Belgium. At the same time, it was the custom for grande cocottes to assume a name which if not actually that of an aristocratic family at least suggested an aristocratic background and the fact that most of these ladies were of extremely humble origins, a fact well known to all their admirers and unmistakable in their behaviour, made no difference. Anne-Marie Chasseigne was transformed into Liane de Pougy; Emilienne d'Alençon's real name is lost in obscurity but the Orleans family were surprised to find they had acquired a kinswoman of very doubtful reputation whose real preferences were for her own sex in spite of her successes as a demi-mondaine — especially with the Belgian king. Leopold's interest in Cléo de Mérode was understandable. As he was a constant visitor to Paris he was well aware of her success in the beauty competition and probably assumed that she had taken the name 'de Mérode' in the same way as so many of his wide range of acquaintances among the cocottes of Paris.

Curious to see this new talent, he arranged for her to be presented to him during a performance of *Aïda* in which she was taking part and he was immediately smitten by her beauty but nonplussed to find that she had every right to the name of de Mérode and obviously was not a demi-mondaine while she on her part, in spite of being slightly over-awed by this meeting with royalty, regarded him as being a very old gentle man — he was over sixty at the time. In any case she was at the time deeply in love with a young man of an aristocratic family which deeply disapproved of his desire to marry a ballet dancer who allowed photographs of herself to be sold all over France and who was in addition reputed to have posed in the nude for Falguière. Cléo and the young man were secretly engaged in spite of the certainty that his family would never consent to their marriage.

Leopold was disappointed to find that Cléo de Mérode was not going to be the easy conquest he had anticipated but still hoped that eventually he would win her interest, and with this aim he paid a visit to the dancer in her mother's apartment but received unmistakable signs that he was wasting his time. This had the disconcerting effect of strengthening the king's passing attraction and extravagant gifts were showered upon her. Driven desperate by her refusals the king declared that he was prepared to install her in greatest luxury in a mansion in Brussels, that he would take steps to ensure that she was treated with the greatest respect, that he would build a theatre in the Belgian capital for her where she would star in sumptuously mounted productions of any ballet she wished. The Belgian ministers became alarmed and a special meeting of parliament was called to deal with this dangerous situation. The king was informed by his advisers that such an action on his part would be against public opinion and could possibly result in a disastrous situation for the monarchy. The Belgian public was prepared to turn a blind eye to his behaviour in Paris but to install his mistress in Brussels was more than they could endure.

Thwarted in this direction, Leopold bombarded Cléo de Mérode with more gifts and letters which she mostly left unanswered. At the same time, it was said that he used Cléo de Mérode as an excuse for visiting Paris when the real purpose of his trip was to discuss with the French Government the delicate questions connected with the appropriation of enormous areas in the Congo without the knowledge of the British

Government who were planning to build a railway from Cairo to the Cape. Inevitably the hopeless royal passion diminished but the gossip flourished and audiences flocked as never before to the opera to see the famous beauty who had enslaved the king and who, most people were firmly convinced, had been his mistress. In addition the exploits of others were added to the story for owing to the similarity of names anecdotes concerning Emilienne d'Alençon and Liane de Pougy were transferred to Cléo de Mérode in particular by English journalists who got the three ladies hopelessly confused. There was ample occasion for gossip for all Paris was fascinated by the exploits of 'Les Trois Grandes' — Emilienne d'Alençon, Liane de Pougy and Caroline Otéro, who headed the official list of ladies available for the entertainment of distinguished guests of the French Government, a rendezvous with Otéro being concealed under the euphemism of 'a visit to the President of the French Senate'.

All three were connected with the theatre but were not remarkable for any exceptional talent in that sphere. Otéro performed extremely energetic Spanish dances — her career had started very obscurely in her native Spain and her name at that time was Puenta Valga but audiences were attracted not so much by her dancing as by her habit of wearing every piece of jewellery she possessed while performing and an awe-inspiring spectacle she must have presented for she had acquired from her admirers an almost unrivalled collection of jewels including a diamond necklace which had belonged to Marie Antoinette, another which had been in the possession of the Empress of Austria and a necklace of matched pearls from the regalia of the Empress Eugenie; ruby, sapphire, emerald and diamond bracelets covered her arms and her rather massive bust supported a fortune in diamond brooches and corsage ornaments. The dresses, coiffures and hats of all 'Les Trois' were the talk and envy of Parisiennes. Otéro had the bodies of her motor cars built with sufficient height and width to accommodate the enormous hats she wore and it is recorded that on one occasion her first trip in a new automobile ended with its turning over at the first corner owing to the carriage being top-heavy. Emilienne d'Alençon had sported a monocle and had started her theatrical career with a troupe of performing rabbits. 'Charming . . . but she lacks inexperience' remarked a critic.

After a whirlwind romance with the young Duc d'Uzès which was ended by his indignant family who discovered that he had presented Emilienne d'Alençon with most of the family jewels, and exiled him to the Congo where the young man died of a tropical fever. The family bought back the jewels and Emilienne d'Alençon granted her favours to Leopold of Belgium. Liane de Pougy, although as acquisitive as the other two, had some pretensions to culture and had a natural elegance of dress and manner which they tried in vain to emulate. Her début in the theatre after an unsuccessful marriage, a bullet in the thigh from her indignant husband and a divorce, was in the rôle of a conjurer's assistant at the Folies-Bergère, to which she invited the Prince of Wales. Amused at the audacity of this unknown performer, His Royal Highness accepted the invitation and approved of what he saw. Liane de Pougy was launched. She had a tendency to fall in love with poets and authors with whom her relationships were stormy and on one occasion culminated in an attempted suicide on her part. In 1910 she married Prince Ghika and to everyone's surprise the marriage was a great success lasting for nearly thirty years when, on the death of the prince, Liane de Pougy retired to a convent and became Sister Marie Madeleine. Emilienne d'Alençon married a jockey who died of drugs in obscurity and poverty. Otéro lived on for many years after her two friends and rivals — the jewellery, so easily obtained, having vanished long since, frittered away or sold to pay gambling debts.

In contrast to these fantastic, slightly unreal characters whose exploits and reputations were wrongly attributed to her, Cléo de Mérode in spite of her growing reputation as a dancer and a famous beauty, lived a comparatively sheltered life, devoted to her mother and deeply in love with Charles, her young nobleman. The increasingly large fees offered to her for solo performances outside the opera ballet enabled her to indulge in the clothes she adored — dresses from Doucet, Chéruit and later Poiret, and hats, lavishly decorated with osprey, bird of paradise and ostrich feathers, from the celebrated milliner Lewis. A number of her hats, dresses and shoes can still be seen in costume collections and give an idea of the elegant figure she must have been, usually dressed in black or some other dark colour. Judging from her photographs she does not seem to have possessed any jewellery of consequence and may have felt that her beauty was at its best when unadorned by jewels.

The state visit to Paris in 1896 of the newly crowned Czar and Czarina of Russia was marked by a gala performance at Versailles when all the greatest talents in Paris were enlisted to honour the presence of the royal visitors upon whom the French Government for political reasons were anxious to make a good impression. The Salon d'Hercule was transformed into a temporary theatre lit by the new electric light which glinted on the sequins of the white dress worn by Sarah Bernhardt as she declaimed in the famous voice an ode written in honour of the illustrious guests. Cléo de Mérode was the soloist in a suite of dances of the period of Louis XIV to the music of Lulli and Rameau and she noticed the air of haunted melancholy which enveloped the royal couple, the Czarina in particular never allowing the faintest smile to disturb her cold, sad beauty.

Cléo de Mérode was pursued more than ever by artists desirous of fixing her beauty on canvas and Boldini at the height of his fame as a fashionable portrait painter asked her to sit for him. She was fascinated by the spectacle of the tiny Italian painter who worked with daemonic energy, dancing away from the canvas to view the model and then rushing back to slash in bold curves and arabesques with long-handled brushes creating by his bravura technique a portrait which gave an almost superhuman chic to his sitters. Far from being exhausted by his labours at the end of a sitting Boldini invariably proceeded to attempt a violent seduction of his model, no matter who they were, and most of his female sitters took the precautions of being accompanied by a chaperon ... some, however, did not.

The numerous offers of engagements she was receiving from managements in America, Germany and other countries,

decided Cléo de Mérode that it was time for her to part
company from the opera ballet which could not afford to pay
her the large fees she was being offered elsewhere. On occasion she returned to the opera to dance a special rôle but until
her retirement her life was to be a continual series of tours
which were tiring but remunerative. She arrived in America to
find the docks in New York plastered with huge signs wel-
coming 'THE MOST BEAUTIFUL WOMAN IN THE WORLD' and was
lavishly entertained by William Randolph Hearst. A tour of
Germany was a triumph where she was hailed as the goddess
of the dance.

In 1899 she suffered a cruel loss, for her beloved mother
succumbed to a long agonising illness diagnosed as cancer.
For six months Cléo de Mérode nursed her mother and after
her death found that all the money she had earned during her
American and German tours had been dissipated in medical
expenses. Too affected by her bereavement to be able to
undertake another arduous tour she accepted an engagement
in Paris at the Théatre des Capucines. Sometime previously
she had seen some pictures of Javanese dancers and decided to
add an Oriental dance to her repertoire as a contrast to the
eighteenth-century and classic numbers she performed. The
theatrical costumier Pascaud designed her a costume which
combined elements of those worn by Javanese and Siamese
dancers and although she had never seen any real dancing of
the Far East her performance captured the feeling of the
native dancing sufficiently to attract the attention of Charles
Lemire, a member of the committee of the 1900 Exhibition,
who was searching for performers for the theatre devoted to
Eastern dancing which he planned to incorporate in the colonial section of the Exhibition. Cléo de Mérode was attracted by
his proposal that she should be the star performer but realised
that a mock Javanese dance performed in a music hall would
not be authentic enough to satisfy Monsieur Lemire, whose
years of residence in French Indo-China had acquainted him
with the real dances of the region. Fortunately there were in
museums a considerable number of Cambodian sculptures of
different periods and from these she was able to reconstruct
typical poses and gestures in addition to details of the appro-

priate costume. The cinema was making its début in Paris at this period and by chance she discovered that a short film was being shown of some Cambodian dancers and this was of great help to her in arranging the choreography of her performance. Her costume on this occasion was designed and made for her by Landolff and was of purple velvet and gold sequins with an elaborate headdress which she found heavy and difficult to balance, but careful as she was to reconstruct the details of the dance and to make her costume as authentic as possible, Mlle de Mérode was not prepared under any circumstances to abandon the famous coiffure. Nobody in the audience could possibly have mistaken her for a Cambodian — she was definitely Cléo de Mérode posing as a Cambodian dancer.

As with all the other evening attractions at the Exhibition, the Cambodian theatre suffered a financial loss owing to the heat-wave that descended on Paris in the summer of 1900, but Cléo de Mérode's Cambodian dance was much admired and she retained it in her repertoire for many years afterwards, performing it in practically every country in Europe and always in the costume and headdress that Landolff had designed.

Life for Cléo de Mérode after the 1900 Exhibition was a combination of great successes, considerable financial reward and hard work. Not long after the death of her mother she suffered another loss when her lover — his surname she never revealed — died while she was on a tour of Scandinavia. She found consolation in her work and for years she, accompanied by a faithful maid companion, toured Europe from Spain to Russia giving solo performances and later pas de deux with Serge Peretti and Rupert Doone. By now the old scandals of her supposed liaison with Leopold of Belgium and the affair of the nude statue were half-forgotten and audiences came to see the beauty and the dancer. How good a dancer she was it is difficult to assess. She was unfortunate in having entered the opera ballet at a time when its artistic reputation and standards were at least mediocre. Contemporary records of her performances are strangely absent in comparison with the many recorded impressions of Loïe Fuller and Isadora Duncan, both of whom Cléo de Mérode saw and admired.

Poets and writers enthused about the divine Loïe and artists and sculptors recorded her magic; time and time again references can be found in autobiographies and reminiscences to the emotional hold that Isadora Duncan had over her audiences who were reduced to tears by the visions of beauty and nobility she evoked. But Cléo de Mérode's ability as a dancer has been completely ignored and she is not even mentioned in books devoted to the history of ballet, a fate shared however by Loïe Fuller. It must be admitted that her repertoire was distinctly limited and would not interest a modern balletomane accustomed to the brilliance of the Diaghilev tradition consisting as it did of Louis XIII pavanes, eighteenth-century minuets, the pizzicato from *Sylvia*, the Cambodian dance and some classical numbers to music by Chopin. A film was made of her in 1900 but she was dissatisfied with the result and it is doubtful if any copies are still in existence.

English v. French

The main source of information about Art Nouveau was *The Studio*, founded in 1893. For a year or so the magazine endeavoured to find a format and a method of presentation. Eventually a formula was decided — and adhered to for the next twenty years — by means of which the readers knew that each number would contain a lavishly illustrated article on a leading painter, another of a more general interest dealing with any subject from domestic architecture to Japanese flower arrangements, several shorter articles on painting or on important exhibitions, and a large section entitled 'Studio Talk' which included smaller notices of provincial exhibitions and articles from correspondents in Paris and Brussels. Occasional notices came from other cities all over the world. The final article was for many years in the form of an imaginary conversation entitled 'The Lay Figure', featuring characters named 'The Man with the Red Tie', 'The Man with a Clay Pipe', 'The R.A.', 'The Craftsman', etc. — symbolic figures who expressed opinions, often hard-hitting, about topics of immediate interest. Presumably written by the editor, these articles, in spite of being written over seventy years ago, are often applicable to the present day.

The critic contributing articles on the current exhibitions in Paris was Gabriel Mourey who had joined the staff of the magazine towards the end of 1894. His first piece was about the patriarch of the official painters, Puvis de Chavannes. After 1902 his name ceases to appear among the list of contributors — by this time he was too prominent a figure in the artistic world of Paris to spare the time to write for *The Studio*. In addition to reviews of exhibitions he often wrote articles devoted to the work of designers associated with Art Nouveau and such opinions as it is possible to disentangle from the

mass of verbiage are often sharply at variance from one issue to another. Unfortunately he suffered from the tendency, common to writers on art on both sides of the Channel, to pad out with sermonising and rhetorical questions which are often completely irrelevant to the subject and to bury one or two interesting and useful pieces of information about the artist in a spate of words. In his shorter pieces he indulges in criticism which is often harsh and contradictory. His comments on Hector Guimard, the architect and designer of the famous entrances to the Metro, which rise in swaying curves like exotic and slightly malevolent vegetation, are so spiteful as to suggest a personal antagonism. Of an interior designed by Guimard he remarks that it is 'in the worst possible taste — fit only for cannibals — nothing more ugly, more pretentious or more inartistic could be conceived; one shudders at the idea of being condemned to live amid horrors such as these.'

In the same article he describes Emile Gallé's works in glass as 'barbarous objects, clumsy and pretentious in conception and realisation alike. It is all in vain that he has become inspired by M. de Montesquiou's infantile verses — for these latter can add no value to articles worthless in themselves.' In the following issue he returns to the attack on Guimard, accusing him of bad taste combined with pretentious ignorance and eccentricity and declaring that though his comments in the previous article may have been strong, they were not strong enough, and proceeds to stigmatise the unfortunate designer even further. Elsewhere in the same issue he boasts of having been asked to leave the exhibition of Tissot's illustrations to the Bible because of his loudly voiced and derogatory opinions. In justice, these opinions were probably justified as Tissot's designs were banal in the extreme and were not enhanced by the poor printing of the English version which was dedicated by the artist to Lord Gladstone. Later he describes some glass by Gallé as 'delicate and subtle as ever'.

There is no question that Gabriel Mourey was on the whole antagonistic to Art Nouveau, though there were occasions when he found something to commend. Unfortunately his spiteful remarks carry more conviction than his lukewarm praise and it would be tempting to ignore him except for the fact that his articles in the most influential English art magazine were the only means by which many people had any acquaintance with the style. Mourey's antagonism to Art Nouveau can be attributed to two causes — he was an ardent admirer of Ruskin and the pre-Raphaelites and hoped to become their prophet in France by promoting their doctrines in his writings and lectures. Art Nouveau he regarded as an interloper, interfering with his plans for proselytising for the William Morris circle. Mourey was thirty years old when Bing opened 'L'Art Nouveau' in 1895, intensely ambitious for power in artistic circles in Paris and anxious to consolidate the reputation he had gained with the success of his book *Passé le Détroit* — the account of a journey to London and the literary and artistic figures he had met in that capital — and of the translations he had made of the poems of Edgar Allan Poe and of Algernon Swinburne. He had also gained admission to the exclusive and influential circle revolving around Edmond de Goncourt who invited him to an evening party at the famous Grenier — a signal honour for a young and aspiring writer. De Goncourt described him as a pallid young man with large dark eyes and a nasal voice — the piercing voice which had caused him to be asked to leave the Tissot exhibition. This entertainment was a week or so after the opening of Bing's new venture which was one of the topics of conversation and no doubt Mourey thought it politic to take his cue from de Goncourt whose personal dislike of Bing must have been even more openly expressed in conversation than in his journals.

The English public — and artists and designers must be included in this category — were on the whole several years behind in their knowledge of contemporary trends in France. It is significant that it was not until a few months after the opening of the 1900 Exhibition that Messrs. Mappin advertised 'New Art' jewellery in the French manner with characteristic floral motifs carried out in coloured enamels and tinted gold. However, these pieces of jewellery were more than likely to have been imported for it was too soon after the opening of the Exhibition to have found designers and craftsmen capable of producing jewellery so different in conception and workmanship from Messrs. Mappin's previously advertised designs of a conventional character of diamonds in geometrical gold settings, which owe nothing to the Arts and Crafts Movement and reflect the current popular taste of the day.

Neither do the French appear to have had any interest in the artistic trends in England and indeed it is difficult to imagine that they would have been particularly impressed even if their acquaintance with the Arts and Crafts Movement had extended further than one small exhibition in Paris and a very occasional article in the French art magazines. To take one example, the settle executed by J. Guthrie from a design by Charles Rennie Mackintosh was praised by *The Studio* as being 'a most pleasant and decorative piece of furniture', but the trade magazine, *The Furniture Gazette*, with a more practical outlook severely criticised the meagre upholstery of stencilled canvas fastened by tintacks and continues to remark that the Arts and Crafts Society must 'expunge this Uriah Heep tendency to use humble accessories'. The French with a long tradition of craftsmanship in upholstery would have regarded such an effort with derision and dismissed it as amateurish.

It is amusing to find that some French critics were also concerned with the moral perversion likely to result from 'Anglo-Saxon' furniture, though this description was applied to the work of the Belgian van de Velde at Bing's 'L'Art Nouveau'. For some reason de Goncourt had a strong prejudice against 'l'étoffe Liberty', a type of thin silk similar in weight to modern Jap silk, which was used a great deal for curtains, for the pleated linings of display cabinets and even more in dress-making—the descriptive captions of fashion plates indicate that the majority of dresses were designed to be made from 'soie Liberty'. Its use, de Goncourt considered, was a certain indication of bad taste and vulgarity but even he did not go so far as his friend the painter Raffaëlli, who was seriously concerned that the rage for Liberty silk would result in an increase in homosexuality.

It is not without significance that Edmond de Goncourt, whose working life is roughly identical with that of William Morris, makes no reference to the latter in his journals and Ruskin is only mentioned once, and then not by name — the entry recounts the story told by Whistler of his case against Ruskin, who is referred to as "an English critic".

The fact that de Goncourt appears to have been unaware of, or at best indifferent to, contemporary English trends does not, of course, necessarily mean that he actually was ignorant of William Morris's existence or his work or that of his followers, but one would have expected someone whose life was mainly devoted to collecting and to writing about the arts to have indicated at some point in forty years of keeping a journal that an influence from England was having an effect in France — if indeed that was the case.

Articles on William Morris by Gabriel Mourey and Jean Lahor began to appear in French periodicals only as late as 1894–95, by which time Art Nouveau as a style was firmly established.

A strong light is thrown on the relationship — or rather lack of relationship — between the English 'Arts and Crafts Movement' and French 'Art Nouveau' by a symposium conducted in *The Magazine of Art* at the comparatively late date of 1904. In a series of four articles thirty-six of the leading figures in the world of art in England including Walter Crane, the President of the Arts and Crafts Society, George Haité, the President of the Society of Designers, G. Aitchison, the Professor of Architecture at the Royal College of Arts, and Aston Webb, the President of the Royal Institute of British Architects, were asked to comment on the proposition 'L'Art Nouveau — What it is and what is thought of it', and to leave no doubt as to what the subject was. The first of the four articles was illustrated with photographs of furniture and objects from Bing's 'L'Art Nouveau' in Paris and from his exhibit at the 1900 Exhibition. The introductory comments in favour of the style were made by F. S. Blizard and must be quoted at some length. He describes Art Nouveau as 'a new arrival' and after quoting some derogatory criticism continues: 'Had the movement been championed by some of our great men in the art world, methinks such criticism would never have been made. But that is just what is lacking — the new style has no long pedigree to recommend it and ensure respect; *it came as a stranger*, and having only its merits to recommend it has been, of course, overlooked to a great extent in consequence.' Blizard continues by declaring that it has had a considerable effect upon the textiles, metal work, pottery, jewellery and furniture 'with excellent results where its interpretation has been entrusted to competent designers'. The style, he declares, 'is replete with beauty of line, grace of form, and freedom, it is a sympathetic style and in its best rendering is full of repose and quiet, unobtrusive beauty. In a word it is art pure and simple, untrammelled by a convention, and therefore in a sense original.' There are two significant points in his remarks. Firstly, that the style 'came as a stranger', implying that it had originally no connection with this country and certainly owed no inspiration to the works or the writings of William Morris and his followers — a claim which Blizard would certainly have put forward to add weight to his arguments. Incidentally, only one of the thirty-six authorities consulted considered that it was connected with William Morris and that exception was Gerald Moira whose work, of all the thirty-six, shows the closest approximation to the Art Nouveau style. Secondly, the date of the symposium was 1904 — a time when the effects of the first big collection of Art Nouveau to be presented to the public — the 1900 Paris Exhibition — were beginning to be felt in this country in the field of design. Blizard's illustrations of Bing's Art Nouveau were more of a reminder than a revelation, for the generous gift of furniture from Bing's exhibit and other sources which had been made by George Donaldson to the South Kensington Museum had caused a storm of protest from the art establishment and had led to their withdrawal from exhibition and almost to the cancellation of the country-wide tour which had been planned for them to acquaint designers in England with the latest developments in Continental design. T. G. Jackson, R.A., who had been one of the leading protestors against the Donaldson gift, repeated his objections and declared that it was 'a mischievous and fashionable craze'. Alfred Gilbert, R.A., stated that he did not know what it was, could not understand it, and while realising that it was hopeless to make himself worthy of Phidias he could not take 'these ephemeral ebullitions of crazy incompetency' in any seriousness considering that they belonged to the young ladies' seminary and the duffer's paradise, ending his comments with the pathetic question: 'Have I understood L'Art Nouveau rightly, or is it still a matter of the grave to which I must come before I understand?' Walter Crane maintained that the new art carried the seeds of dissolution within itself — that originally it had some very remarkable and original work but that the forms were not always understood by those who used them and were abused by commercial imitators. He saw its origins as having traces of decadence, primitive motives, attenuated pre-Raphaelitism and Japanese influence — he was the only one to detect the connection between Art Nouveau and Japanese art. Voysey considered Art Nouveau to be 'distinctly unhealthy and revolting . . . void of intuition . . . no sign of reverence — atheism, conceit and apish imitation seem to be the chief features . . . not worthy to be called a style. It is not,' he concludes, 'merely the work of a lot of imitators with nothing but mad eccentricity as a guide; good men, no doubt, misled into thinking that art is a debauch of sensuous feeling, instead of the expression of human thought and feeling combined and governed by reverence for something higher than human nature?'

George Clausen, R.A., did not like the style, questioning whether it was not a continuation of the baroque and quotes Alfred Gilbert's fountain in Piccadilly Circus (often referred to as a piece of English Art Nouveau by later writers) as an example of what Art Nouveau was not — controlled by a fine taste. George Framton, R.A., confessed to ignorance of the subject but thought that Art Nouveau was made on the Continent and used by parents and others to frighten naughty children, which he thought was a bad practice and far worse than the old English bogyman. Art Nouveau opposed all Marcus Stone's convictions and he classed it with Walpole Gothic and the Chinese architecture of the Brighton Pavilion as 'unlovely, meaningless and uncomfortable'. Luke Fildes, R.A., declared flatly that 'newness of art' did not interest him. Reginald Blomfield maintained that Blizard was quite mistaken in thinking that the style 'came as a stranger' for it had started some twenty years before with the 'ingenious experiments of two young architects with an uncommon share of eccentric ability, who for the first time revealed the numerous possibilities of the 'swirl' and the 'blob'. The names of these two pioneers Blomfield does not reveal but he goes on to describe how their work attracted attention in Germany and Austria and finally reached France from whence it was returning to the country of its origin. W. D. Caröe was of the opinion that Art Nouveau was the 'work of the hothouse, the forcing bed, which a clean and manly nature may endure for a time, but which cannot thrive upon'.

Enough has been quoted to demonstrate clearly that the leading English painters, architects and designers, some of them pupils or followers of William Morris, condemned the Art Nouveau style with one or two exceptions and even then the interest was only lukewarm. The interesting feature of all the remarks, even those which were not entirely unfavourable, is that they showed a complete detachment with no indication that any of them, with the possible exception of Blomfield and his claims for his anonymous architects, perceived the remotest connection between Art Nouveau and English design. Art Nouveau was apparently regarded in artistic circles as another example of French folly and eccentricity, dangerous and probably immoral.

In the same year — 1904 — *The Studio* also enquired: 'What is meant by Art Nouveau?' in its monthly feature, 'The Lay Figure'. 'The Man in the Red Tie' who made a regular appearance in the articles as an advocate of the more *avant-garde* tendencies defined Art Nouveau as 'an inspired protest against the absurd survivals from past centuries, which have too long hampered the progress of art . . . the revolt of intelli-

Agathon Léonard: 'Cothurne'.
Gilt bronze version of the
biscuit figures modelled for
the Sèvres factory.

Hippolyte Lucas: portrait of
Loïe Fuller. Oil painting.

G. Flamand: bronze figure of a dancer. *A photograph exists of Liane de Pougy in a similar attitude and this may have been the inspiration for the figure illustrated.*

Raoul Larche: gilt bronze lamp in the form of Loïe Fuller dancing.

'*Le Palais de L'Electricité et le Château d'Eau*': one of the most striking
buildings at the *Paris Exhibition* especially at night when the illuminated
fountains were said to have created an unforgettable impression.

Eugène Colonna: drawing room designed for Bing's 'Art Nouveau' at the Paris Exhibition of 1900.

Gaillard: dining room designed for Bing's 'Art Nouveau' at the Paris Exhibition of 1900.

Georges de Feure: dressing room designed for Bing's 'Art Nouveau' at the Paris Exhibition of 1900.

Georges de Feure: boudoir designed for Bing's 'Art Nouveau' at the Paris Exhibition of 1900.

Frank Brangwyn: 'La Danse'. This panel and its pendant were painted by Brangwyn for the entrance foyer of Bing's 'L'Art Nouveau', 22 Rue de Provence, Paris. 1895.

gence against the tyranny of convention' and another of the
dramatis personae of the articles, 'The Designer', declared it to
be neither decadent nor revolutionary but 'simply modern'. It
is interesting that *The Studio* after featuring articles on Art
Nouveau for ten years — only using the name after the opening
of Bing's establishment in 1895, however — should decide to
pose the question as to the nature of the style at a time when
the principal designers in France had begun to move away
from Art Nouveau and when the two main advocates of Art
Nouveau, Bing the impresario, and Gallé, possibly its leading
exponent, were passing from the scene. The mere fact that the
question was posed at all implies an ignorance on the part of
the readers of *The Studio* as to the nature of Art Nouveau
even after years of propaganda on its behalf by the editor and
staff of the magazine.

English critics would really have been shocked had they
seen the extraordinary furniture created by the sculptor
Rupert Carabin. The use of the human figure as a decorative
element in furniture was not, of course, new and had been
widespread in Europe from the seventeenth century onwards;
the Italians, with their tradition of sculpture, had made use of
it in its more exotic aspects as the many examples of carved
and painted Negroes used as supports for consoles and tor-
chères, culminating in Andrea Boustolon's fantastic chairs and
tables which swarmed with exuberant putti and blackamoors.
The classic revival featured the more impersonal figures of
caryatids used as supports for side-tables, but these, like the
earlier examples, were purely decorative and impression is
given of living human beings having been used as models.
The famous side-table created by Dalou for La Païva, which is
now in the Musée des Arts Decoratifs in Paris, shows a new
trend, however, for the two asymmetric bronze figures of
crouching youths which support the massive top could have
been modelled from life. Carabin leaves us in no doubt that
living models were used for his furniture. The women who
clamber over his furniture are hardly idealised at all, they
could be Degas ballet dancers or seamstresses with no clothes
on. After posing for Degas for one of his bathing pictures, the
models went on to Carabin's studio to pose for him. These are

naked women playing with Persian cats—not idealised decorative symbols of women, and this fact gives a disturbingly sensual impression—almost fetishistic—to his furniture. Carabin's chair was intended to be used for reading de Sade's *Justine* or Huysmann's *A Rebours*, and his table to carry volumes illustrated by Félicien Rops or Japanese pornography.

Carabin was the creator of the elaborate showcases in the Musée Galliéra which was opened in 1894 to house a permanent collection of contemporary sculpture and works of art—paintings were not admitted. The elegant building in the classic eighteenth-century style by the architect Ginain was erected at a cost of four and a half million francs and was named after the Duchesse de Galliéra who had paid three and a half million francs for the site. The director appointed, Charles Fromentin, was empowered to purchase examples of

ON N A QUE SOI

FERNAND KHNOPFF 91

the finest craftsmanship of the day and, aided by grants from the government, collected pottery by Carriès, glass by Gallé and Tiffany, which were accommodated in the vitrines upheld by Carabin's nude women, considered by some to be unsuitable as they distracted attention from the objects. The particular treasure of the Musée Galliéra was a bust of Victor Hugo by Rodin. The Galliéra collection no longer exists as a unity and the gallery is now given over to exhibitions.

From 1894, a year after the appearance of *The Studio*, Ferdinand Khnopff was a regular contributor to the magazine, writing articles on Belgian artists and news of various exhibitions in Brussels, Liége and other towns. His cool, dispassionate reporting was in great contrast to the passionate prejudices of the irascible French correspondent, Gabriel Mourey, and he continued to be the source of information about the artistic life in Belgium for years after Mourey had ceased to write for *The Studio*.

His factual reporting is a reflection of his own paintings, concerning which a critic, writing in 1893, made the prophecy that they would bring to the artist as great a fame in England as that enjoyed by Alma Tadema, and not only fame but a knighthood. That this prophecy was unfulfilled can be attributed to the fact that Khnopff found no attraction in settling in England but also to the melancholy almost morbid disposition of the artist. He was born in 1858 of an aristocratic family and spent his childhood at Bruges. The atmosphere of this romantically melancholy town, its canals thick with green weeds, among which the swans floated, its brick buildings when the silence, in the days before the invasions of charabancs loaded with tourists, was broken only by the carillons of bells, made an indelible impression on a sensitive child, although he was too young to appreciate the treasures of mediaeval paintings to be found there. His father's appointment to an important post in the Brussels Court of Appeal necessitated the family's moving to the capital, and on leaving school Khnopff was enrolled in a law school, much against his will. In 1876 his parents, realising that he had no aptitude for legal studies, allowed him to join the Academie des Beaux Arts and he also became the only pupil of Xavier Mallory. He soon attracted attention with his individual style of painting, which owed something to his admiration for Burne-Jones and to an interest in Japanese art — he had a large collection of masks and fans.

Khnopff's studio on the outskirts of Brussels was built to his own design and was surrounded by a magnificent rose garden, which provided a contrast to the severe lines of the building, which was often taken for a vault or a chapel. The black entrance door, under a lintel inscribed with the words 'Past — Future' opened on an entrance hall with walls of white polished stucco, the only decoration being a stuffed peacock, a small Greek statue on a slender blue column and a replica of one of Khnopff's most celebrated paintings, 'The Blue Wing'. A grey-blue curtain gave access to a white corridor,

windowless, but indirectly lit by stained glass panels of blue and gold which cast a mysterious glow on the walls on which were inscribed in gold letters, 'Everything comes to him who waits'. This corridor led to a white room sparsely furnished with some white enamelled chairs and a small table bearing a delicate Venetian glass vase containing a single white flower — a décor calculated not to distract attention from the artist's paintings. This room was used by Khnopff as a dining room on the rare occasions when this solitary and reserved artist could bring himself to entertain intruders from the outside world. A staircase from this room led to the main studio, the lofty walls of which were painted, the lower half white, the upper portion and the ceiling a deep blue with gold-painted decorations of conventionalised floral design. A white marble pool containing mother-of-pearl shells emphasised the bare white mosaic floor, and the absence of any furniture beyond easels supporting finished works as well as the painting currently in progress. His studio, unlike so many of the period which were usually so cluttered with Italian Renaissance furniture, Moorish tables, that it is difficult to see how the artist found room to paint, was almost empty. But scattered about the room, however, were a number of objects; some valuable, a pair of bronze chimeras, a Tiffany glass cabinet, or a beautiful Japanese kimono; some simply for their decorative effect — a branch of withered mistletoe, a brilliant blue butterfly or a plaster cast. No lover of animals, Khnopff had been given a tortoise, but finding it too noisy he had banished it to the rose garden where he found it some time later, quite dead. Overcome with remorse, he had the unfortunate beast cast in bronze by Lalique and, for ever silent, it once more found a place in the studio. Curtained off from the studio was a large minstrel gallery — called the Blue Room — which was used by Khnopff as a place of relaxation after working, a soothing environment where he could rest his eyes on original drawings and paintings by the painters he admired — Delacroix, Gustave Moreau and Burne-Jones.

Apart from designing the scenery and costumes for productions of *Parsifal*, *Oberon*, and *Le Roi Arthur* at the Théâtre de la Monnaie at Brussels and painting a number of portraits, Khnopff's work was dedicated to the portrayal of a mysterious woman who appears in various guises in practically all his paintings. She was reported to be his only model, to be English and even to be his wife, married secretly and kept in complete seclusion, hidden from the world which was allowed to see only her painted representations, usually in a tight-fitting dress with long sleeves and a high collar, her hair dressed closely to her head and sometimes with a wreath of dried laurels. Her delicately marked eyebrows, large pale eyes, small mouth and full chin, for some reason inspired a French critic to describe her as having an 'English' face. He made a portrait of her as a tinted ivory mask encircled with bronze and enamel leaves, and with a garland of flowers; this was exhibited in 1897.

She appears time and time again standing erect in her pale dress, gazing out of the canvas beyond the spectator, wrapt in an introspective reverie; sometimes in the painting there is

included one of Khnopff's favourite studio properties — a cast of the classic head, 'Sleep', She is never shown in movement, all is stillness and silence, and the pallid tones of bleached wood, stone or marble. In one painting, 'The Scent', she is shown touching with a gloved hand the ivory mask which Khnopff had made of her. In 'Solitude' she sits in a black version of her usual dress, holding a sword, at her feet an iris with a miniature version of 'Sleep'.

The truth was perhaps even stranger than the surmises which were made about the identity of this strange woman who seemed to obsess the painter. In fact, she did not exist at all, except in the imagination of Ferdinand Khnopff, but to him she was so real that he could over a period of years paint her portrait in a myriad versions so consistently that it is difficult to realise that he did not use a living model. When asked by a curious visitor if he would ever marry this woman should he ever meet her living prototype, he replied that it would be the last thing he would do for he would know too well what she was thinking — an explanation of the extraordinary painting he did of her head superimposed on the body of an eagle, transforming her into a harpy.

Khnopff was a regular exhibitor at the 'Geste Esthétique' organised by the self-styled 'Sâr' Peladan, leader of the Rose and Croix brotherhood. Joséphin Peladan, a devotee of the more mystic aspects of catholicism, was convinced that his family stretched back in an uninterrupted line to Babylon and that one of his ancestors, a Babylonian king, had appeared to him and had given him the title of Sâr or Magi. In 1874 his first book, *Le Vice Suprême*, appeared and in it he propounded the ideology which was to absorb him for the rest of his life. One must, he declared, love Beauty more than self and must defend it at all costs, for beauty represented the Ideal and even sexual love must be avoided in pursuit of the Ideal. From 1885 to 1908 he wrote no less than nineteen volumes on this theme; the members of the Order of the Rose and Croix were required to swear an oath in the name of Leonardo da Vinci that they would seek, admire or love the Beautiful: those who could not believe in more than art and science were allowed only a black-and-rose coloured robe, while those who adored the Eucharistic Presence were permitted to wear blue. In 1892, Sâr Paladan organised the first Salon du Rose and Croix at the Durand Ruel Gallery and the rules governing the exhibits are worth quoting in full. Sâr Peladan gave the artists an unlimited choice of subjects with certain exceptions. No historical or prosaic subjects and all representations of manual labour, no patriotic or military subjects, no representation of modern life, no portraits unless the sitter had unusual beauty or great spiritual qualities (portraits of Sâr Peladan himself, although he lacked unusual beauty, were permitted and indeed encouraged), no rustic scenes, no landscapes except those in the style of Poussin, no sailors or anything connected with the sea, no comic subjects, and finally, no Oriental subjects. However, in spite of the oath to avoid sexual love and never to seek poesy in women, it was noted by a critic that a great many paintings of female nudes were in evidence. As might be expected, the standard was not high in spite of such names as Bourdelle, Jean Dampt, Aman-Jean and Felix Valloton among the exhibitors, and the public found the exhibition a source of considerable amusement. Undeterred, the Sâr organised another show the following year at the

Champ de Mars and continued to do so for a number of years — each exhibition at a different gallery.

Why such a considerable artist as Ferdinand Khnopff should have associated himself with this semi-mystic, semi-erotic fraternity is a mystery, but he seems to have had a genuine admiration for Sâr Peladan; his paintings actually conform to the requirements of the Leader and at the same time achieve a mysterious and singular atmosphere.

A Flower . . .

A flower—an excellent guide for the decoration of porcelain, furniture, fabrics or costume. Free and growing out of the earth, or captive in a vase, it presents an artist with the perfect example of the universal creative force—in it he may find form, colour and even expression, a mysterious expression composed of stillness, silence, and the fugitive beauty of things which are born only to die in the same moment. Their frail organisms can be the joy and despair of an artist as much as the most majestic creations of the universe, combining as they do the infinity of a landscape, the beauty of the human face, the sparkle in an eye or the mystery of a smile.

Gustave Geoffroy

In their efforts to create a 'new art' and to disassociate themselves from the styles of the past, designers at the end of the nineteenth century turned with one accord to Nature as a source of inspiration. Since the 1870s, Emile Gallé had been preaching and practising his tenets that Truth and Beauty could only be found in the forms of natural growth, that as each generation must find its own formulae of design the only true fount of ideas was to be found in the never-ending marvels of natural objects. Furniture, he maintained, should be made for use but decorated for pleasure, and that decoration should be drawn from Nature. Lessons had been learnt from

Japanese art, that of the asymmetrical arrangements of decorative motifs and that of formalising the shapes of leaves and flowers in a new way to European eyes, paying less attention to the realistic interpretation of vegetation than to a stressing of its linear and abstract decorative qualities. Rare and exotic varieties of paeonies, irises and chrysanthemums were imported from Japan and with them came the Japanese gardeners with their knowledge of Oriental horticulture. Not always, however, did they find France the equivalent of a bed of roses. The anonymous Japanese gardener attached to the household of the beautiful Comtesse de Greffuhle came to her cousin, Robert de Montesquieu, with the pathetic story that the Comtesse had given instructions that economy must be observed, with the consequence that the poor man had been fed by the housekeeper on an exclusive diet of rabbit for two years. Debilitated by this, the gardener appealed to Montesquieu for help and was promptly engaged on the spot with a promise of a more varied menu. In addition to these rare and costly blooms brought with great difficulty from the Far East, humbler indigenous flowers were used as sources for decorative effects—often for the first time. Naturally the national flowers of Lorraine, the thistle and the myosotis were popular with designers centred in Nancy, the former appearing on a number of pieces of furniture by Gallé either inlaid or carved in relief and often accompanied by the Cross of Lorraine the latter scattering its delicate blue blossoms over vases by Daum. The flowers and herbs of the countryside and the country garden were glorified in glass or metal — rosemary, lavender, clematis, vines of grapes or hops, masturtiums, daisies and in particular the dandelion whose diaphanous seed-head was a favourite with jewellers. The poppy, both wild and cultivated, offered endless scope to designers with its brilliant colour and the linear possibilities of the crinkled petals. Together with its poppy-head it could be used as a symbol of sleep or, more darkly, hint at the feverish dreams induced by opium. The seed pods of the prolific sycamore were used many times by both Lalique and Mucha, as were the similarly shaped leaves and berries of mistletoe. Mucha utilised the leaves and pendant blossoms of the datura, said to be poisonous, in several designs for light fittings, the flower with its curling points concealing the electric light bulbs. The maidenhair fern and honesty were transformed into lace as a decoration for fans. Sweetpeas, lilac and cornflowers became as popular as the rose and the lily which had held sway for so long and Gallé, not content with the flowers of his day, recreated the flowers of the prehistoric ages from fossils.

Lalique found that flowers carved in horn, the material he had made popular, were set off by the addition of insects and particularly beetles, finely made of gold, their wing cases enamelled or set with tiny rubies or diamonds whose glitter sparkled against the pale sheen of the horn. Mucha designed a border of the sinister stag-beetle combined with poppies, which he included in his *Documents Decoratifs*; it was also to be found on Gallé's vases.

One might have expected that the butterfly would have been a natural accompaniment to the flowers depicted, or used as an element on its own. But it was 'La Libellule', the dragonfly, which for the first time enjoyed a brief spell of popularity as a decorative object. Dragonflies transformed to gold and enamel by René Lalique and lesser jewellers and a new mythological character, half-woman, half-dragonfly, joined the ranks of centaurs and sphinxes. Women's heads, torsos and bodies were combined with the iridescent wings of the insect, suitable companions to the 'femmes-fleuris' and the flower maidens of Klingsor's magic garden. Dragonflies appeared on

Emile Gallé's vases, some as though they had just settled and some as though they were sinking into the glass to be preserved for ever like flies in amber. An elegant woman could go to a costume ball arrayed as a dragonfly, confident that she

would look beautiful and be generally admired. Fans, buckles and combs became dragonflies, and the climax of the Carnival of Flowers at Nice was the appearance of 'Madame Libellule', a huge figure of a woman with, of course, the wings of a dragonfly, her dress cut very low, a monocle in one eye and seated on a gigantic lobster This 'Libellule' mania can partly be attributed to the appearance in 1885 of a volume, *Poems de la Libellule* translated from the Japanese by Judith Gautier, the younger daughter of Théophile Gautier, and Ernesta Grisi the dancer. A precocious child, Judith and her older sister were taught Chinese at an early age.

When she was sixteen, Judith married Catulle Mendés in spite of the opposition of her father, who refused to allow Mendés to enter his house for many years in spite of the efforts of reconciliation of Judith, who had been and still remained his favourite child. In the following year, 1867, she published, under the nom-de-plume of Judith Walter, her first book *Le Lion de Jade*, an adaptation of Chinese poems. In addition to being talented as a writer and a linguist, Judith Mendés was also beautiful; in 1873 Edmond de Goncourt, accompanied by Gustave Flaubert, attended the funeral of

Victor Hugo's son François and at the gate of Père Lachaise
cemetery he met Judith Mendés, her mother and Tsing, her
Chinese language teacher, and was impressed by her sphinx-
like beauty, her white skin, enormous eyes with thick black
lashes, framed by a feather boa and enhanced by the contrast
with her mother's lined monkey face and that of the Chinese.
The strangeness of the encounter was heightened by Judith's
mentioning casually that she was on her way to a lesson in
magic. But neither beauty nor magic could ensure the fidelity
of Mendés who had formed a liaison with a rich Irish girl,
Augusta Holmes, by whom he had five children — ample
reason for the legal separation which Judith obtained in 1878
which left her free to indulge her enthusiasm for the Orient
and for Wagner.

Her apartment, decorated with Chinese embroideries,
Japanese fan paintings and lanterns, and always great bowls of
paeonies or flowering trees, was a meeting place for writers
and artists. Robert de Montesquieu was an intimate of hers
and one of his poems, 'Haute Classe' in his volume *Florilège*, is
dedicated to Judith Gautier. Passionately fond of animals, she
had a black cat called Satan and a chihuahua, Biblis, given her
by Pierre Loüys.

Judith Gautier was not averse to leaving the perfumed and
poetic atmosphere of her apartment to indulge in a profitable
job of journalism, especially when the occasion was one with
Oriental associations. She wrote a glowing description of the
acting of Sada Yacco for *Femina* and in a professional capacity
was a guest at the Chinese ball given by Pierre Loti on May
4, 1903. The Gothic staircase, the stained glass windows and
crystal chandeliers of the Loti house at Rochefort-sur-Mer
may have been a slightly incongruous setting for the entrance
of 'the young Empress Ou-Tse-Tien' but there could be no
doubt as to the authenticity of the magnificent Chinese robes
and uniforms worn by the hundreds of guests who spared no
effort in falling in with the wishes of their hosts that Chinese
costume should be worn and as Judith Gautier commented
when describing the occasion later, 'Who could imagine that
so many authentic, luxurious Chinese costumes of all periods
and provinces could be found in the West?' However

Madame Loti appeared in a Japanese kimono — beautiful but Japanese — and it was explained that she was quite correct in doing so as it closely resembled the robes worn in China in former times. She received her guests — the Chinese minister regretted being otherwise engaged but sent his nephew and an attaché in his place — accompanied by her niece, Mlle Duvigneau, who was dressed as a Chinese dancer and was a little downcast, having planned to perform a classic piece, 'Dancing on the Golden Lotus', but failed to find either a golden lotus or anyone to teach her the steps. Incidentally, the guests had nearly been mobbed as they arrived, for a huge crowd of sightseers had gathered to watch the arrivals and had caused great embarrassment by poking their heads in the carriage windows and commenting loudly on the masqueraders — even by striking matches and lighting candles to see better, and the gendarmes who had been drawn to the spot by the noise and confusion were barely able to control the crowd and make a way for the carriages to enter.

When they finally and safely arrived, however, the guests were dazzled by the spectacle; every variation of actual Chinese court costume was to be seen, satins and velvets of every colour richly embroidered, headdresses of pearly jade, kingfisher feathers or peacock feathers, carved and painted fans . . . the women wore black wigs, the men either wearing the round hats of mandarins with long pigtails attached, or their own hair dyed black. The garden was lighted by Chinese lanterns and the odour of opium came from a grotto where a number of hired actors were simulating the raptures of dreams induced by the 'benevolent poison'.

Promptly at ten o'clock the 'Empress' made her entrance. A soldier in full Chinese armour appeared, bearing a red lacquered sign worded 'Be silent', in Chinese characters, followed by the Imperial musicians playing 'The Procession of the Clouds' in a variety of flutes and drums. Four guards then appeared in red satin robes embroidered with gold dragons and rainbows and bearing fly-whisks, preceding the Master of Ceremonies, carrying a whip and flanked by two lines of soldiers with lances, banners and insignias. Two guards with headdresses of eagle feathers bore a purple satin baldaquin decorated with peacock feathers, and as the music grew louder the 'Empress' made her entrance and proceeded down the main staircase, resplendent in her robes copied from those worn by her T'ang dynasty original—gold embroidered with pheasants and dragons, a golden headdress representing a phoenix with outstretched wings from which long tassels of pearls descended, framing the pale, impassive face of the unknown Chinese girl who was for one night the reincarnation of a long-dead Empress. Her attendants carried huge fans of crane feathers, a handmaiden in green satin embroidered with roses carried the Imperial pet dog who wore his yellow satin coat with a dignity and aloofness equal to that of his mistress. Eunuchs (not of course real), servants and soldiers completed the procession, which wound its way through the house among the awestruck and admiring guests to the Throne Room, where a magnificent Chinese couch placed before an elaborate, carved screen awaited the 'Empress' and where amid clouds of incense she received the homage of the guests who after paying their respects made their way to the mediaeval gallery where they found the buffet, no doubt very welcome by this time. The entertainment went on until dawn when the two Chinese guests, who it was remarked looked less Oriental than anybody, departed for Paris politely complimenting Pierre Loti with the comment that they felt as though they were leaving China for the second time.

Especially exotic was the Louis XV fête given in 1901 by the Maharajah of Kapurtala, not in Paris but in his palace of Mussooric in the Himalaya Mountains. His governess, Mlle Meillon, had instilled in him admiration for all things French and he rather imagined himself as an Indian reincarnation of Louis XV. Two hundred guests were invited to the magnificent if remote palace which was brilliantly lit by electricity for the occasion. The European guests, mostly English, were in eighteenth-century costume, or what passed for it at the time; the women added a few touches to their very 1900 evening dresses, wore a white wig with an ostrich feather somewhere, while the men were uncomfortable in velvet coats, knee breeches and white wigs which looked incongruous above heavily-moustached faces. The Indian guests wisely wore their

own magnificent costumes but the four unfortunate sons of
the Maharajah were dressed in tiny eighteenth-century suits
and unfortunately fuzzy white periwigs framing their little
dark faces, with enormous languorous eyes. Lavish favours
were showered on the guests, a necklace of diamonds and
sapphires to the most beautiful guest — at least, the lady the
Maharajah thought the most beautiful, while a coffer of jewels
was given to the one the guests thought the most lovely. Eight
couples danced a minuet and were rewarded with jewels by
the delighted Maharajah, who was enchanted at this strange
re-creation of the glories of Versailles on a Himalayan moun-
tain top.

In 1903 the Baronne de la Tombeth invited the guests to
her fancy dress ball to attend wearing costumes representing
Parisian shops or products. The hostess, a rather homely lady,
looked like a mature Ophelia in a dress strewn with flowers
and a card, worn like a tiara, announced that she represented a
florist called 'Aux Mille Fleurs'. Blooker's Cocoa was seen
chatting to Ripolin Paint, and one lady must have got a little
tired of announcing that her costume represented 'Aux
couleurs solides de Raffaëlli'. Confusion was caused by two
ladies, one 'A la Brioche de la Lune' and the other 'A la
renommée de la Brioche' which was added to by two more
ladies who had the same idea of appearing as the iridescent
pottery made at Golfe Juan by Clément Massier. A dignified
elderly gentleman in the full regalia of a Doge, carrying a model
gondola, was 'Le Carnaval de Venise' and escorted his wife, who
wore a large artist's palette complete with brushes as a
headdress to indicate that she represented 'La Palette d'Or'.

Various Japanese shops, 'L'Etoile d'Orient', 'Mikado' and
'Au Soleil Levant' were the themes of other costumes, and the
toyshops such as 'Aux Parades des Enfants' gave opportunities for a number of heavily moustached gentlemen to appear
in incongruous disguises. After a period of identification and
mutual admiration, the guests settled down to the real purpose
of the evening's entertainment, which was to indulge in the
new and sensational dance which had been first performed at the
Nouveau Cirque by the Americans, Mr. and Mrs. Elks — the
cakewalk, to the tune of 'Joyeux Nègres' by Rudolphe Berger.

The
Flowery Kingdoms
of Madeleine and Louise

In view of the popularity of flower paintings at this period, it is surprising to find that contemporary writers praise the portraits of Fantin-Latour and enthuse over his mythological compositions such as 'Siegfried et les filles du Rhin', 'Venus et ses Amours', and hail him as one of the finest contemporary painters of the nude while virtually ignoring his flower paintings. Jacques-Emile Blanche declared that hardly anyone in France was aware of the fact that Fantin-Latour painted flowers, that without showing them to anyone he packed them up and sent them by the crate load to Mrs. Edwin Edwards in London, who acted as an agent between the artist and the English and American admirers of his portraits of flowers.

Had his countrymen been aware of Fantin-Latour's talent for flower painting, they might not have lavished such excessive praise upon the work of Madeleine Lemaire who was regarded as 'one of the most universally esteemed women artists' and whose indefatigable production of flower paintings in most media earned her the title of Professor of the Museum of Natural History—the first woman to be granted this honour. Reproductions of her paintings are reminiscent of the sprays of flowers which were to be painted on the satin tops of boxes of expensive chocolates, and at a guess her fame was due more to her position as one of the leading hostesses of the day than to her talents as an artist, which were considerable enough, however, to ensure that not only did she sell every drawing or painting that she executed, but also that she was in the enviable position of having a waiting list of eager buyers, finally achieving a Legion d'Honneur in 1906.

This imposing and influential figure in French society, friend and hostess to all the prominent names in art and literature, was born Madeleine-Jeanne Coll in 1845. She became a pupil of, firstly, a Madame Hybolin, then of the fashionable portrait painter Charles Chaplin, 'The French Tiepolo', an Englishman who had adopted French nationality and whose success was envied by Manet. After her début at the Salon of 1846, Madeleine Coll surged forward triumphantly; at some point the 'queen of roses' acquired a husband who appears either to have died quickly or was content to remain so much in the background that he is never mentioned. Her contribution to the Salon of 1877 received an honourable mention, and about the same time a daughter, Suzanne, was born — she also followed in her mother's floral footsteps and they frequently exhibited paintings together. Madame Lemaire was now set on her careers as an artist and hostess, neither career interfering with the other; in fact, each was mutually beneficial. Her costume parties at her home in the rue Monceau became famous; in 1888 the guests were bidden to appear in costumes made of paper, while at another in 1900 she chose the theme of the Universal Exhibition, appearing herself as 'La Porte Monumentale de l'Exposition' in a remarkable dress in the Empire style, shading from a dark hem and train to a pale high waistline, the skirt of the robe being embroidered with a large lily. On her head Madame Lemaire wore an extraordinary headdress of a small model of the famous portal by Binot, topped by a tiny reproduction of the statue 'La Parisienne' and flanked by a pair of wobbling Eiffel Towers complete with flags. Suzanne Lemaire wore a dress representing Electricity, and looked very pretty. As a compliment to their hostess, three of her guests, Mesdames Blumenthal, Brun and Trousseau, decided to go as a fan decorated by Madeleine Lemaire, all in flower costumes and headdresses and holding an enormous folding silk fan, signed by Madame Lemaire, behind their heads. Later in the same year, in the magazine *Femina*, Madame Lemaire wrote an article on the correct way of decorating a silk fan in watercolours with a spray of flowers. Dressed in a loose peignoir encrusted with lace, a highly unsuitable garment for the work in hand, Madame Lemaire was shown performing the various stages from arranging the flowers as models to admiring the finished result.

Madeleine Lemaire was not unhandsome, with high-arched eyebrows and heavily-lidded eyes — although the size of her nose and the recession of her chin became more noticeable as she grew older — and her expression, amiable in photographs, could harden, the eyelids droop in the disdain of a society hostess when she considered a guest had broken her rules. The mischief-making Jacques-Emile Blanche was banished from her 'Tuesdays' — he achieved the dubious record of being barred by two other hostesses in the same week. But Marcel Proust was favoured and Madame Lemaire decorated an early book of his, *Les Plaisirs et Les Jours*, with drawings of roses, much to the gratitude of the budding author.

She decorated with yellow roses the silk train of an elegant black sequin-embroidered evening dress, which was presented by the readers of *Femina* to the exiled Queen of Madagascar in 1901 at a reception — Madame Lemaire naturally being the hostess.

Very different, although they mixed in the same social circles, was a rival painter, Louise Abbéma, a short, tailored lady with cropped hair upon whom the wiser mothers with young daughters kept a wary eye. Some fourteen years younger than Madeleine Lemaire, she had also been a pupil of Chaplin and of two other fashionable portrait painters, Henner and Carolus-Duran, and made her début at the Salon of 1896 with a portrait of Sarah Bernhardt, whose inseparable companion she became for many years, even after the advent of a younger rival, the actress Sarita. Curiously, she and Bernhardt, in later years began to resemble each other, and the actress in 'L'Aiglon' could be mistaken for the painter in her studio. Her range of painting was greater than that of the feminine Madeleine Lemaire who could manage a life-size portrait but preferred painting a fan. Louise Abbéma, in a tailor-made with a starched collar and cravat held by a jewelled tiepin, thought nothing of covering large wall spaces, and her diminutive figure clambered briskly up and down ladders while she painted murals in the 'maieries' of several districts of Paris, in the Hôtel de Ville, in, naturally, the Théâtre Sarah Bernhardt and the Governor's Palace at Dakar.

On December 9, 1896, Sarah Bernhardt was honoured by a luncheon at the Grand Hotel followed by a performance at the Théâtre de la Renaissance, when Madame Bernhardt performed, before an audience made up of the most illustrious figures drawn from society and the worlds of the theatre, literature and art, the second act of *Phédre* and the fourth act of *Rome Vaincue*, subsequently being crowned with laurels while five eminent poets acclaimed verses written in her honour for the occasion, which was commemorated by a Golden Book, limited to six hundred numbered copies. Inevitably, Louise Abbéma played an important part in organising the occasion and a full page was devoted to a reproduction of her drawing of Madame Bernhardt in her most famous plays, *La*

Princesse Lointaine, Lorenzaccio and *Le Passant.* The famous medallist Alexandre Charpentier decorated the cover with a nymph holding laurel sprays — a design carried out in gauffrage, a method adapted from Japanese examples, by means of which the design is raised in a slight relief on the surface of the paper. René Lalique, who had designed jewels for Bernhardt, created an exquisite medallion in gold depicting the actress in profile and this was reproduced as a frontispiece. Carolus-Duran, Gervex, Mucha, Benjamin Constant, La Gandara, Granie and Rochegrosse contributed drawings and lithographs to be reproduced alongside poems by Coppée, Catulle Mendés, Rostand and José Maria de Heredia. Few actresses have received such a singular demonstration of admiration. Louise Abbéma and Madame Lemaire had a race for official honours, ending in a draw when Abbéma became a Chevalier de la Legion d'Honneur in 1906.

Until the last decades of the nineteenth century any young woman aspiring to be an artist had little opportunity of receiving the professional tuition available to men. In fact, her only chance of doing so was to become the pupil of an established painter and to work in his studio. If in time she showed sufficient ability she might be allowed to work on the less important sections of a painting he was engaged upon, but even after receiving a lengthy tuition from one or more painters her chances of exhibiting her work were limited. Eventually the two most important art schools in Paris, L'Académie Julian and the Beaux-Arts opened their doors to women students, and before long it was accepted that an art class should include a proportion of female students, not only French but English, American and even Japanese. Entry was comparatively easy at the Académie Julian as long as the student could pay the fees of 100 francs a month or 700 francs a year. Classes went on from 8 a.m. until 10 p.m. although only the most enthusiastic worked at that intensity, most students, particularly the women, preferring to work in the mornings and again in the evenings, leaving the afternoons free for domestic duties and buying food. Students were only allowed in the life classes after they had shown their proficiency at drawing from plaster casts and female students could, if they chose, avoid the embarrassment of drawing from the nude model in the company of male students by joining classes for women only—with the male models decorously draped. Every student had to submit examples of progress once a week and five or six times a year a competition was held where the work of male and female students was judged together. Mixed classes were supervised by a male and a female 'massier', a senior student who not only acted as a chaperone (female students were permitted to bring a chaperone of their own in any case) but in addition posed the model and was responsible for orderly behaviour in the classes.

The rules of entry to the Beaux-Arts were stricter— prospective female students must be French and between the ages of fifteen and thirty, and her chances of gaining admission were seven out of a possible five hundred. On the other hand, if she were successful she stood an equal chance with the men of gaining the coveted Prix de Rome, which was practically a guarantee of eventual success and official honours.

No restrictions were placed on women copying the paintings in the Louvre and other collections—a valuable source of income for an indigent student finding difficulty in paying fees at an art school. No such consideration worried the pupils at Madame Perrée, who ran a successful private studio for young society women not particularly interested in becoming professional artists but desirous of completing their education and acquiring an agreeable method of passing the time. The indefatigable Madeleine Lemaire passed on the secrets of painting flowers to numerous pupils, while Aman-Jean's studio was devoted to young American ladies who flocked to him for tuition as a result of the portraits of millionaires and their families he executed on trips to the United States.

Very few of these women painters achieved more than a mediocre standard and one of the more onerous duties of critics was to attend the annual 'Salon des Femmes Peintres' which had been inaugurated in 1881. 'They would be better employed in devoting themselves to embroidery,' sighed one critic, 'but there is no use in telling them—they will do it.'

The Divine Loïe

On October 20, 1891, a new play called *Dr. Quack, M.D.* was presented in New York after a provincial tour. The audience was only mildly expectant for word had come from those who had seen it on tour that the play itself was to say the least mediocre but there had also been talk of a new dancer — and nobody seemed to know her name — who had appeared in a scene which had been added during the tour in an attempt at improvement. When the curtain rose the stage was empty except for the figure of a man in evening dress who stood in a green light. He began to make hypnotic passes and suddenly from out of the shadows a mysterious impalpable figure appeared — that of a girl wrapped in a gauze drapery who appeared to be under the spell of the man and obeyed his commands, fluttering and floating in the eerie green radiance, appearing and disappearing in half shadows and transforming herself into vague shapes now suggesting a butterfly, now a flower. The scene was very short but it made a deep impression on the audience and when the curtain dropped there was a storm of applause which unfortunately did not happen again that evening for the play, after the brief but exciting prologue, was a disappointment. During the interval the audience searched their programmes for the name of the dancer but without success — some may have noted the name of Loïe Fuller in a minor rôle but as she was moderately well known as a soubrette nobody imagined that it could be she. But it was indeed Loïe Fuller and neither she nor anyone else in that audience could have guessed that it was the beginning of an extraordinary career that would make her internationally famous and transform her into the living embodiment of 'Art Nouveau'.

Like her contemporary *Charley's Aunt* Loïe Fuller was no ordinary woman and even the circumstances of her birth were unusual, for she made her entry into the world in the exceptionally severe winter of 1862 in the small town of Fullersburg a few miles north of Chicago. Her parents about whom little is known lived in rather straitened circumstances some distance from the town and as the time of the approaching birth drew near her father grew increasingly worried about his wife's health for all his efforts to keep the house reasonably warm had failed. He managed to get his wife to the only tavern in Fullersburg which was owned by some cousins and where the public room had a large stove and there huddled in blankets for even there the cold was so intense that a pan of water six feet away from the stove froze solid — Mrs. Fuller gave birth to a daughter who was christened Mary Louise.

She was a precocious child who loved to recite in public at church meetings and sewing-bees and is reputed to have made her début at the age of two and a half with a travelling repertory company probably as little Willie in *East Lynne*. She seems to have adopted a theatrical career at an early age and the mundane Mary Louise became the more exotic Loïe. In later years she was curiously reticent about her early life. Apart from mentioning him in connection with the circumstances of her birth she never again referred to her father. She was very close to her mother who accompanied her on her tours in later years and she had at least one brother.

Her theatrical career was moderately successful; she travelled in various companies in America and the West Indies, toured with Buffalo Bill and even managed her own companies, appearing in one of them in London, and it was there that the first contribution to her later career was made. One evening she was at a dinner party and found herself seated between two young officers who were on leave from service in India. During the course of conversation one of the officers announced that he would send her a present when he returned to India. She had forgotten the incident when some months later she received a parcel containing a length of the finest silk which was made into a very full skirt, but having no use for it at the time she put it away. Not long after when she returned to the United States she was engaged to play a small part in *Dr. Quack, M.D.* which was to have a trial tour before being presented on Broadway. During the tour the producer had the idea of adding a prologue which would show in mime the effects of hypnotism and thus set the mood for the piece. The stage was to be completely empty lit only by a green glow from the footlights. She had been chosen to appear in this scene though nothing had been decided as to what she should actually do and in addition she had been asked to improvise a costume. She remembered the Indian silk skirt which the English officer had sent her. Trying it on she found that it was much too long for her so she put the waist band round her neck improvised a high waisted effect with long full sleeves. The semi-transparent silk floating and shimmering around her created a magical effect in the dim light and its fullness concealed the fact that it was her first attempt at dancing. In spite of her later fame as a dancer Loïe Fuller never had any training as a dancer and the only lesson she had in her life was when a small boy tried to teach her the Highland Fling when she was a little girl and gave up in disgust at her clumsiness.

Dr. Quack, M.D. soon failed but the success of her appearance in the prologue gave her the idea of developing her performance and presenting it as an act in itself. She was not the first 'Skirt Dancer' by any means but the accidental combination of lighting and the Indian skirt had given a new twist to what was ordinarily a commonplace music-hall turn.

The months that followed were discouraging. For hours each day she practised in front of a mirror experimenting and discovering new effects. She found that a thin bamboo rod held in each hand and covered with yards of silk which were extensions of her dress gave her a wider range of effect though the effort of controlling the silk in movement caused her excruciating pain in her arms and shoulders, straining muscles which were unused to such strenuous exertion. She was, after all, thirty years old — not an ideal age to begin a dancing career and in addition to this she had to invent her own technique as she went along. Although her performances, as she admitted, contained a great deal of improvisation, she had to repeat the theme of a dance and to submit to the discipline of the music. The physical exertion of starting as a dancer at an age when most dancers are at the peak of their powers took its toll in time — she was twice threatened with paralysis of the arms and often had to be carried off the stage in a state of prostration at the end of her performance.

She began to be interested in lighting effects when she was practising in her room and a shaft of sunlight from the half-drawn curtains fell across the silk she was agitating. At this time lighting effects in the theatre were comparatively simple as most theatres were lit by gas — it was Loïe Fuller's good fortune that electric lighting was just beginning to be introduced in the theatre.

Another discouragement was that as she made the rounds of the theatrical agents trying to interest them in her new project she found that they refused to contemplate the idea of her as a dancer. They knew her as an actress and were willing to offer her parts as an actress but were not interested in doing anything for her as a dancer particularly as they knew very well that she had no training or experience and were not impressed by the *Dr. Quack, M.D.* episode for as her name had not been on the programme they were sceptical that it was she who had had that small success.

When her small savings had almost disappeared she found an agent who grudgingly consented to give her an audition — she suspected that he was doing it more from pity than because he expected to be able to do anything for her. With no music and with none of the lighting effects she needed Loïe Fuller danced for him and in a few moments his indifference turned to enthusiasm. He suggested a piece of music for her dance — Gillet's *Loin du Bal* (later it would be Beethoven, Chopin, Schubert and Debussy); he encouraged her to build up a repertoire and, most important, he found her engagements. The months of loneliness and discouragement were over but another worry appeared and one which was to stay with her for many years. As her success became more widespread so the imitators began to appear — even as she was dancing at one theatre someone else would be doing a bad imitation of her at a theatre nearby even in one case going to the length of using her name on the posters.

For some reason she had the *idée fixe* that she would achieve her greatest success in Paris although she had never been there and did not speak a word of French — even after spending years in the French capital she could only speak a few words and those with an atrocious accent. When she was offered an engagement in Hamburg she saw it as a stepping stone to her ambition and without bothering to find out what the engagement comprised she set out with her mother for Germany. When she arrived she found that she was to appear in a disreputable music-hall and after a few days her manager absconded and her mother fell gravely ill. An epidemic of cholera had broken out in Hamburg. Her mother was taken to a pest-house in spite of her protests but the illness was diagnosed, not as cholera but as a nervous complaint which was to render her a permanent invalid. Desperate with worry and once more penniless Loïe Fuller was rescued by a chance meeting with an impresario who had heard of her work and he found her a series of engagements in Altona, the pleasure park of Hamburg. There followed a humiliating engagement in Cologne where she found herself performing in a circus preceded by an educated donkey and followed by a troupe of elephants.

In spite of these hardships she persevered, inventing new effects and practising incessantly until she had perfect control over the yards of silk. She was continually experimenting with lighting. One night when she was dancing in the beams of light from two spotlights, a drunken electrician put the wrong colour in the lamp he was supposed to be controlling so that she was gyrating in a multi-coloured light — an effect she was quick to adapt. She became intoxicated with coloured light and the magical effects it produced on her draperies and on one occasion she became so fascinated by the beauty of red light that completely oblivious of the audience she stopped her dance and stood lifting her arms up and down completely absorbed in the play of light on silk.

From Cologne she made her way to Paris where her intuition
that she would find her great success proved to be correct.
After some difficulty — nothing to what she had been
through — she was engaged by the Folies Bergère. Success was
immediate and sensational. Paris had a new star and artists
had a new source of inspiration. With the technical resources
of a theatre which was based more on spectacle than on talent,
she was able to realise all the effects that she had dreamed of
since that first appearance behind a simple row of green footlights. She danced on a glass floor lit from below — a startling
novelty at that time. She danced on a stage surrounded with
huge sheets of mirror so that the audience had not one but
many Loïe Fullers. Her repertoire increased and her taste in
music improved. She danced as a Lily, as Fire, as the
Firmamant, Night, a Bird, an Archangel, a Butterfly, a
Midnight Moth . . . Each new dance was a theatrical event
and a closely guarded secret until the first performance, for
she was still harassed by imitators, all inferior and by their
inferiority damaging to her reputation. The only imitation of
her dances which she allowed was that given by her own
sister-in-law and she was only permitted to perform in conveniently distant places like Russia and South America. Even her
dresses were made in secret and when she created her
Serpentine Dance each panel of the enormously full skirt was
given to a different artist to paint so that nobody could copy
the complete dress. The care she expended on her stage
costumes did not extend to her private life for she was completely indifferent to fashion or to her appearance outside the
theatre. Marie Curie found her 'an odd, badly dressed girl
with a Kalmuck face innocent of make-up, her eyes blue as a
baby's' while Jean Cocteau, writing thirty years afterwards,
remembered her as a 'large American woman, rather ugly and
bespectacled'. Allowing for differing standards of beauty the
impression to be got from her photographs is of a vivacious,
rather pretty woman who became noticeably plump as the
years advanced.

But the artists of the day were less concerned with her looks
than with the beautiful effects she could produce and with the
poetry and magic of her performance. She personified what

artists felt about Woman as an abstraction — a vague tantalising ethereal vision.

Jules Chéret's posters for her had a firmness and strength missing from his modish pastiches; Raoul Larche captured the flickering delicacy of her creations in bronze and most appropriately incorporated an electric light in his evocation of a creature enamoured of light; Whistler and William Nicholson drew her; Hippolyte Lucas portrayed her a little idealistically and certainly less draped than she was in life and achieved a painting better than any of his work at the Monte Carlo Casino. She was called 'The Queen of all the Dancers' and the Parisian shops were full of Loïe Fuller hats, Loïe Fuller shoes, Loïe Fuller ribbons and Loïe Fuller petticoats.

During her second season at the Folies Bergère a charming incident occurred. Many years before when Loïe Fuller was sixteen years old and still an unknown struggling actress, Sarah Bernhardt had paid a visit to New York where she was received like royalty. Every seat at every performance was sold months ahead. A group of the leading players in New York petitioned Sarah Bernhardt to give a special performance for the theatrical profession only at which they could pay tribute to her art. Bernhardt graciously consented. Loïe Fuller's standing in the profession was too negligible for her to be able to claim a seat at this performance with any confidence but she was determined to be present and managed by sheer persistence to buttonhole the manager of the theatre and pleaded to be allowed to stand at the back of the auditorium — anywhere it would be possible for her to catch a glimpse of her idol and to hear the famous golden voice. Harassed as he was by the demands already being made on him the manager was touched by the young girl's sincerity and he gave her two passes — one for her and another for her mother. The reception given to Bernhardt that evening was delirious — at her first entrance she was applauded for half an hour before she was allowed to speak and by the end of the evening the audience was in a frenzy of enthusiasm.

Now the position was reversed and it was Sarah Bernhardt who was begging for a seat at one of her performances. She was installed in a box accompanied by her grandson and the message was sent to Loïe Fuller in her dressing room that Mme Bernhardt was in the theatre. When she made her first entrance she could hardly move for nervous excitement but she soon gained control over her emotion and forgetting the rest of the audience she danced for Bernhardt alone. At the end of the performance Bernhardt stood up in her box to applaud and the audience fell silent, awestruck at the sight of the Goddess of the Drama paying tribute to the Goddess of the Dance.

Loïe Fuller is often mistakenly referred to as being inspired by the paintings on Greek vases and as being responsible for a revival of Greek or rather pseudo-Greek dancing. This is not borne out by the facts for not only was the spectacle that she presented completely alien to the subjects portrayed in Greek art but she herself never referred to Greek art in any way or seemed to have any interest in the subject — in fact she never set foot inside a museum until she came to Europe and by that time the idea of her dancing was complete, capable of refinement and polish through the more advanced theatrical techniques of lighting she found in Europe but not capable of being influenced by a culture with which she had no sympathy. Not for her were the emotional ecstasies over Greek vases and Tanagra statuettes indulged in by Isadora Duncan. Her source of inspiration was light itself and the magical effects it could produce on a thousand yards of agitated silk — without electric lighting there could have been no Loïe Fuller. Her interest in anything that could enhance the effects she desired was avid. Reading that a Madame Curie and her husband had discovered a new substance that glowed in the dark, her reaction was not wonder at a new scientific discovery — her busy mind knew that this was just what she needed for a new dance she had in mind in which she would appear as a phosphorescent butterfly fluttering on a darkened stage. She wrote to the Curies asking them if they could make her a radium dress. Considerably amused Madame Curie wrote back explaining at some length why such an idea was not very practical. To show her gratitude for Madame Curie's kind and courteous reply she decided to repay them by giving a performance for them alone. This she achieved by invading their house with an army of workmen and technicians and transforming their dining room into a miniature theatre where she performed her entire repertoire. She became a devoted friend and admirer of the Curies and introduced them to Rodin who had been sketching her.

When the plans were being made for the Universal Exhibition which was to be held in Paris in 1900 Loïe Fuller had the idea of building her own theatre as part of the Exhibition. The design was entrusted to Henri Sauvage (who was also designing a marionette theatre) in collaboration with the sculptor Pierre Roche, a pupil of Falguière. The curved façade was modelled with conventionalised draperies in plaster, the centre entrance being flanked by two lifesize portraits of the dancer which seem to emerge from the draperies. The sloping roof rose to a series of dormer windows with curved tops which echo the curves of the façade and between these windows were corbels alternating with smiling portraits of La Loïe. No detailed description of the decoration of the interior has survived but it was draped in blue-grey velvet with concealed lighting.

Pierre Roche was a devoted admirer of the dancer and sculpted her many times in various phases of her performance. He had an original and inventive mind—one of his ideas was that drivers of the new automobiles should wear light papier-mache masks which could be versions of their own features and incorporate glass panels to protect their eyes from the dust—a more elegant substitute for the conventional goggles. He was the inventor of a process of illustration called Gypsography by means of which paper was stamped in very low relief in a design and then emphasised with delicate touches of water-colour. He used this process in a rare volume written in praise of Loïe Fuller by Roger Marx, the Minister of Fine Arts and an expert on medals. Marx and his young sons were devoted admirers of Loïe Fuller and the elder boy wrote a poem in her praise when he was eight years old.

> Pale vision
> A l'horizon
> En ce lieu sombre
> Fugitive ombre . . .

Devant mes yeux vague
Une forme vague,
Suis-je fascine?
Une blanche vague.

En volutes d'argent
Sur l'ocean immense,
Elle court follement,
Elle s'enfuit et danse.

Protee reste! Ne fuis pas!
Sur la fleur qu'on ne voit pas
Palpite, hesite et se pose
Un papillon vert et rose:

Il voltige sans aucun bruit
Etend ses ailes polychromes
Et maintenant c'est un arum
Au lieu d'un papillon de nuit . . .

During the course of the Exhibition Loïe Fuller not only danced in her charming theatre herself but also presented the famous Japanese actress Sada Yacco and her company in a play written by Mme Yacco's husband Kawakami. It was a financial disaster for its sponsor but its artistic success may have consoled her. Sada Yacco appeared the same year in London at the Coronet Theatre. She was an anomaly in the classic Japanese theatre. Originally trained as a geisha, she met, fell in love with and finally married the actor-poet Kawakami who was at that time the director of a theatre built in the European style in Tokio and where classical plays were presented by a traditionally all-male company. There were also companies which were entirely female but for Sada Yacco to join her husband's company and to be the only female in an all-male company was a break with tradition which caused a great scandal. In addition Kawakami had subversive opinions and political ambitions which got him into trouble with the authorities so that he had to leave Japan very hurriedly with his wife. He found a haven in America where he was joined by most of his company.

His was not the only Japanese troupe presenting NO plays in Europe at that time for Loïe Fuller later rescued the female star of another company who had been stranded in Marseilles with no money and speaking no word of French. The practical difficulties of these little bands of actors must have been considerable — the problem of communication not being the least for there could have been very few people in Europe with any knowledge of the Japanese language. On one occasion the literary world of Paris decided to give a luncheon in honour of Kawakami. Loïe Fuller, whose French was elementary, was asked to interpret — presumably the organisers of the luncheon imagined that as she was the impresario for the Japanese company she must be able to speak the language. Fulsome and elaborate speeches were made in praise of the author who sat impassively while La Loïe solemnly 'translated' into an Oriental sounding gibberish and then interpreted his reply in her halting French. As she really understood very little of the French speeches and nothing at all of the Japanese speeches it must have been an exhausting meal for her but everyone appeared to be satisfied.

The vehicle for Sada Yacco's triumph was a play *La Geisha et le Chevalier* which in its original version lasted for fourteen hours but which was reduced to two hours for European consumption; but even this abbreviated version gave Paris a picture of a feudal Japan which had begun to disappear when that country was opened to the West some thirty years before. Charles Ricketts, the painter and collector, saw Sada Yacco in London and described her as 'Entrancing; curiously natural in her acting, she also at times lapses into vague entranced movements of the eyes — a downward squint — odd marionette movements of the arms. Marvellously graceful and elastic in movement she does, or allows to be done to her, astonishingly violent things. As a dancer she has a wild 'electric' grace, something of a wave or a tiger by Hokusai'.

On one occasion Sada Yacco played Portia in *The Merchant of Venice* whether in English or Japanese is not recorded but the performance was described by Judith Gautier as a 'surprise'.

Loïe Fuller's career went from one triumph to another; she danced before most of the royalties of the period with two notable exceptions — Queen Victoria and the Dowager Empress of China. Both had expressed a desire to see her. A contract in America prevented her coming to England to perform before the former while the serious illness of her mother made the trip to Peking and the Imperial Palace an impossibility — it was not until many years later that she learnt that a high ranking mandarin had been disgraced by the Dowager Empress for his failure to produce the dancer and the breakdown in negotiations.

Isadora Duncan was for a very short time part of her troupe but the result was unhappy and ended in bitter scenes and accusations of ingratitude. The two dancers, one at the height of her fame and the other at the threshold of notoriety, were antipathetic to each other in every way. Though Loïe Fuller had a genuine desire to help the young Isadora Duncan's career she was not in sympathy with the latter's passion for 'Greek' dancing which she regarded as an excuse for performing as near nude as possible. Duncan, bursting with youthful health and vitality and blatantly heterosexual, was scornful of the older woman's adoring circle of female disciples and impatient with her physical weaknesses which she regarded as hypochondria. Each referred to the other in guardedly derogatory terms in her autobiography and the impression is left that a great deal more could have been said.

Loïe Fuller enjoyed an artistic success with her own performances and her presentation of Sada Yacco but like most of the impressarios of the theatres attached to the Exhibition found herself heavily in debt when the time came to close the Exhibition. Such a great star was not lacking in offers however and the most remunerative was one for a long but arduous tour of Germany. Among the dancers she recruited for the supporting company was Isadora Duncan, already beginning to be recognised as an artist. Loïe Fuller's efforts to draw the attention of influential patrons to Duncan's talents as a dancer on the German tour were unremitting and through the introductions and the solo performances which Loïe Fuller arranged Isadora Duncan's path to the heights of fame was made considerably easier, not that the younger woman displayed much gratitude for in after years she denied, on one occasion, ever have met Loïe Fuller, though she did acknowledge her existance in rather spiteful terms in her autobiography.

The years that followed were filled with ceaseless activity for 'La Loïe'. For some time she made her home in England, was the author of 'The Japanese Girl' presented at the Duke of York's Theatre in 1907 and in the following year appeared at the Hippodrome Theatre in a ballet 'Light'. But she was no longer a young woman and as the years advanced the physical strain of her performances coupled with a tendency to overweight led her to devote more time to her school of dancing. In 1919 the critic Emile Vuillermox, evaluating the talents which had contributed to modern dancing classed Loïe Fuller, Isidora (*sic*) Duncan and Jeanne Ronsay (a now forgotten dancer who also ran a school in Paris) as 'the three great improvisers' who had given as much inspiration to their contemporaries as Nijinsky or Karsavina in the field of the classical ballet. Loïe Fuller's restless energy and passion for experimenting in new forms of expression were still as strong as ever and in 1924 she collaborated with Gaby Sorère in making an experimental film 'Le Lys de la Vie' which was shot partly in silhouette and had some sequences which were projected in the negative.

The following year saw the long postponed Paris Exhibition of 1925 and — still known to Parisians as 'The Divine Loïe' — she created a ballet 'La Fleuve' which was danced by her pupils. This formed part of the nightly entertainments given in the Exhibition and Loïe Fuller's thoughts must have turned to the theatre named after her which, not far away in distance but very far in terms of social changes, had been one of the attractions of that long summer twenty-five years before.

Finis

The heat wave which lasted throughout the torrid summer of
1900 to the discomfort of the visitors to the Exhibition finally
broke and the autumnal mists enshrouded the fantastic
buildings which had glittered and shimmered in the almost
tropical air. The alien trees and plants, so carefully tended and
watered by a host of gardeners began to shed their leaves and
the inhabitants of the native villages shivered in the chill
autumn air. November came and the Exhibition was closed
to the public. The treasures which had dazzled the public
were carefully packed for return to their sources while workmen began to demolish the buildings which had been the
cause of so much anxiety for M. Picard a few months before.
In spite of an agitation that the Exhibition should be repeated
the following year the vast elaborate pavilions enshrining the
decorative arts, the industrial arts, science and commerce from
practically every country in the world, the restaurants, the
native villages and the enormous fun fair ended their brief
existance in a débris of broken plaster and shattered timbers.
Bing's elegant 'Art Nouveau', Loïe Fuller's little theatre and
the Cambodian temple where Cléo de Mérode performed
disappeared without trace and only a few faded photographs
are left to record their being. With them vanished the Japanese
gardens, the Madagascan jungle, the elaborate parterres of
flowers. The rare trees were torn up and fragile exotic blooms
trampled underfoot in the frenzy of demolition. The trottoir
roulant was torn down and with it disappeared the hopes of

those who had envisaged it as the 'pavement of the future' though truncated versions of it were used in subsequent exhibitions. The Egyptian belly-dancers, the inhabitants of the native villages and ex-Queen Ranavalona's Royal Orchestra presumably found their ways home—the fate of Chérie, the elephant is not recorded.

With the closing of the Exhibition the interest of designers in the Art Nouveau seems to have waned. Bing, according to Jacques-Emile Blanche 'grew weary of the struggle and retired' handing over the management of his gallery to his son in 1902 when it reverted to the sale of Oriental antiquities and exhibitions of contemporary paintings—it was still in existence in the 1920s. Thus many of the creative artists lost an outlet and a showplace for their work although a number of Bing's protégés exhibited at the rival firm 'La Maison Moderne' before it also closed a short time after. The exact date of the closing of 'La Maison Moderne' is unknown. The Nancy school lost its guiding hand in 1904 when Emile Gallé died after a long illness. Victor Prouvé his friend and collaborator of many years was elected as leader of the school but his interests were mainly directed toward sculpture and he lacked the inspiration and guidance which Gallé had provided. Majorelle, however, continued to produce furniture in the Art Nouveau manner of great elegance, mainly for private clients, for a number of years prior to 1914. The illustrations in catalogues of exhibitions of the decorative arts held in Paris show that artifacts in the Art Nouveau style were extant until about 1905 although a number of these may have actually been made some years before. In the ways that such things happen Art Nouveau seems simply to have gone out of fashion in the early 1900s and a contributory cause for this may have been the flood of ill-designed, sentimental examples of debased Art Nouveau resulting from the Exhibition. That this change in fashion was sudden is indicated by Roger Allard in an article on modern furniture in 'Feuillets d'Art' for 1919 when he comments that 'the krach (*sic*) of the modern style of 1900 whose monstrous flowering poisoned French art explains the state of mind of modern manufacturers who are loath to exploit any new tendency' for fear of financial loss.

Art Nouveau was finally swept aside by a tide of Orientalism of a more sensuous kind than that which had contributed so much of its inception. The ethereal elegance of Japanese art was superseded by the more barbaric attractions of a legendary Persia or Arabia, of roses, or minarets against a purple sky, pearl-decked, veiled odalisques — all the trappings of the world of Haroun-al-Raschid to which the French were introduced by Dr. Mardrus in his translations of *The Thousand and One Nights* published between 1898 and 1904. This exotic décor struck a responsive chord with many French artists and designers for whom a sketching trip to Algeria was considered a necessary part of their artistic education and the architecture of Moslem North Africa was close enough to that of Baghdad to spark off their imaginations. Sheherazade began to replace Mélisande and Ondine as an ideal of feminine allure.

One of the first manifestations of this can be seen in 'Figaro Illustré' for 1900 — an oriental pastiche 'La Belle sans Nom' by Jean Rameau with illustrations in colour by Manuel Orazzi which combine the swirling lines and arabesques of hair and the smoke of incense, so typical of Art Nouveau, with the repertoire of Oriental motifs which were to become so much a part of the work of Paul Poiret and Léon Bakst.

Bibliography

Cléo de Mérode, *Le Ballet de ma Vie*, Ed. Pierre Horay, Paris, 1955.

Edmond et Jules de Goncourt, *Memoires de la Vie Litteraire*, Fasquelle et Flammarion, Paris, 1956.

Jacques Émile-Blanche, *La Pêche aux Souvenirs*, Flammarion, Paris, 1949.

Jacques Émile-Blanche, *Les Arts Plastiques*, Les Editions de France, Paris, 1934.

The Studio.

Art et Décoration.

L'Art Décoratif.

Les Industries Artistiques à l'Exposition Universelle de 1900.

Figaro Illustré.

Der Moderne Stil, Stuttgart, 1899.

Le Théatre

The Artist.

Robert de Montesquiou-Fezansac, *Le Chef des Odeurs Suaves*, 1894.

Robert de Montesquiou-Fezansac, *Les Hortensias Bleus*, Paris, 1908.

Loïe Fuller, *Quinze Ans de ma Vie*, Librairie Félix Juven, Paris, 1908.

Souvenir of the Fine Art Section of the Franco-British Exhibition 1908.

'The Studio' Year Books of Decorative Art.

Femina.

Documents sur l'art Industriel au xxe siécle, Editions de la Maison Moderne, Paris, 1901.

The Magazine of Art.

'*Self-Portrait*', Charles Ricketts, R.A., Peter Davies 1939.

Index